THE MAGIC CURTAIN

THE MAGIC CURTAIN:

The Mexican-American

Border in Fiction, Film,

and Song

by Thomas Torrans

Texas Christian University Press

Fort Worth

Library of Congress Cataloging-in-Publication Data

Torrans, Thomas.

The magic curtain: the Mexican-American border in fiction, film, and song / by Thomas Torrans.

p. cm.

Includes bibliographical references and index.

ISBN 0-87565-257-3 (alk. paper)

1. American literature—Mexican-American Border Region—History and criticism. 2. Mexican-American Border Region—Songs and music—History and criticism. 3. Mexican-American Border Region—In motion pictures. 4. Mexican-American Border Region—In literature. 5. Mexican-American Border Region—Civilization. I. Title.

PS277 .T67 2002

810.9'9721--dc21

2002002298

Ya me despido de Juárez,
de la Frontera también;
ya el Gobierno nos dió pases,
ya nos vamos en el tren.

Now I'm parting company with Juárez,
And the border country too;
Now the government's given us passes,
Now we're off on the next train through.

—*Corrido de la triste situación*
(Ballad of the Sad Situation)

CONTENTS

Part One:

The Background

1

The End of an Era

Much water has, quite literally, passed under the bridge since the Rio Grande began to epitomize the border between the United States of America and the Republic of Mexico, the long boundary line extending westward to the Pacific notwithstanding. Around that time the population along the whole great sweep of the borderlands was sparse, spread out as thin as charity. Native American groups still prevailed in some border areas, while in others a coyote, as it was said, could barely make a living. By and large, the desert prevailed. It still does.

Yet in less than a century, at a time when transportation meant by horse, and years were measured by the seemingly endless Mexican Revolution that threatened to spill across the border onto U.S. soil, transportation means jet-speed air travel, and time computed in nanoseconds. The border population is counted in millions, and cleanly run factories that are antiseptic marvels of the computer revolution and the electronics era are counted in the thousands along the Mexican frontier.

It is not surprising that many view all of this as the future. In fact, the further shape of things to come has been assembling here for several decades. Obeisance is to the new god of high technology; allegiance increasingly to the global corporation, the multinational conglomerate. But component assembly plants are dispersible, perhaps as fluid as the Great River, as mobile as the desert sands.

Meanwhile, other avenues of commerce flourish, for all borders have their rendezvous with clandestine cargoes. Boundaries of nation-states are always venues for contraband: drugs, illegal immigrants, fake documents, hijacked goods, hazardous wastes, reproductions of articles infringing copyrights and patents. With time, imbalances in almost any human endeavor are grist for the smuggler's mill.

There is not so much that is new in all of that apart from the widespread expansion and mushrooming increase in such activities, greatly abetted, of course, by the tremendous growth in population and the spiraling spread of new technologies. When the Mexican-American border was less populated and less technologized, it was more easily romanticized in song and story. But folklore and fiction fall away before an onslaught of data, some of which are true. And the Information Age reflects different facets of reality. An era has vanished, and the stage set for a new one. For a while, though, the sorcerer's curtain is lifted and the magical realm it enfolded can be glimpsed.

2

Gateway of the Underdog

In one of the classic films of escape, *The Getaway*, the bank-robber couple not only get away with the money but also with what obviously will be a new and better life awaiting them below the border in Mexico. Toward the end of Sam Peckinpah's 1972 movie, Doc and Carol McCoy (Steve McQueen and Ali MacGraw) finally have made it. After harrowing escapades of running gunfights and car chases they are temporarily on foot, but with a satchelful of hard-won American money.

Extracting only a few bills from their wealth of stolen loot is enough to overwhelm a passing border character, a Mexican-American type, whose dilapidated pickup truck they offer to buy. Apparently it is a princely sum for such a rattletrap. Joyously overcome by his sudden stroke of good fortune, the man turns over the key to the jalopy. If he now is the one suddenly become a pedestrian on the lonely highway, it is worth it to have come across such a bonanza. With folding money in his pocket it's easy enough to walk away from such a marvelous transaction.

Manna from heaven indeed—one can almost read his thoughts: a couple of crazy gringos with no more than a valise between them but, who can say, seemingly so much in love perhaps that they can barely wait to cross the border and get to Mexico. Romantic Mexico. It's hard enough to make it on the American side of the border country; only Americans with more money than sense and madly enamored of one another might want to go there. Escape there.

To the local, former pickup owner, despite the magicality of the moment it must seem incomprehensible, as baffling as grand passion itself. No doubt only he can be aware that what awaits them on the other side of the boundary is even less than what their present surroundings afford—a treeless area, semidesert, an immense stretch of open country dominated by a boundless, and empty, horizon.

Certainly there is not much else in sight: dust and wind and blowing tumbleweeds; and suddenly an astonishing quietude after a long space of violence, chattering gunfights and careening car chases. In the broken-down pickup Doc and Carol and valise rattle off toward the border. There is no reason to doubt they will not make it, and with their fortune intact—McQueen has well established Doc's uncanny ability to survive as well as to hang on to their bagful of riches. The camera fades out on the edge of the grand escape across the magic curtain that enfolds the border country.

The seeming immensity of it all, this gateway to Mexico and to the United States, perhaps it is that which makes it also appear to be seemingly endless, heavily populated in only scattered oases but many of those now plush watering holes and cosmopolitan centers of commerce—a lot of it illegal. But legend and romance and derring-do exploits are the stuff it is made of, the borderland of bewitchment, of enchanting dreams, even of grim reality. It's Marty Robbins singing about how "Out in the West Texas town of El Paso, I fell in love with a Mexican girl." But it's also the ancient anonymous ballad of *The Cowboy's Lament,* also known as *The Dying Cowboy* or simply *The Streets of Laredo*, taken from the opening line, "As I walked out in the streets of Laredo," which might lose much of its forceful character were it set somewhere else; the border town lends strength to the fatality, the nonchalance and indifference to death.

The border country, after all, is where all the Robin Hood-like adventures of the Cisco Kid took place in an array of old Hollywood "B" pictures, even a televised series. And while Cisco may dally at times in romantic interludes, he always dashes back in time to right wrongs and gallop away to new adventures. Cisco remains a sort of twentieth-century Don Quixote with his ever-faithful general factotum and sidekick as a properly Mexican Sancho Panza. He is the proper leavening for Cisco's bravado, the two of them quite at home ranging the whole expansive sweep of the magic curtain of the border, the gateway to escape, just as it becomes in *The Getaway*.

There is, of course, big money at stake in *The Getaway*, and it is obvious that on the other side of the boundary that rises and falls like a magic curtain the loot will buy much more than it ever could in the country of its origin. Poverty has always been a rampant fact of life along the entire border, even from the days of the original Cisco Kid created by the short-story writer O. Henry (William Sidney Porter) in the early 1900s. The difference, on either side, is largely one of degree, of subtle gradation. Simply being poor in one place may be only a thin line between utter destitution in another.

And while items of contraband, even stolen money, change with the times, there is always money to be made from smuggling whatever may be most currently in demand, whether those be products or people themselves. If for decades the demand on one side was for capital, then on the other it might be for cheap labor. If for a while it was for stolen livestock, it might later be for armaments or automobiles. If it later was for agricultural workers, later it might be for housemaids or prostitutes or assemblers in light industrial and manufacturing plants.

Eventually the bigger demand would come—for marijuana, sundry pharmaceuticals, even placebos, and for drugs, particularly for drugs, mostly cocaine. And with it would come a harder band of traffickers, of contrabandists. The border country was still the land of the magic curtain but no longer was the whole backdrop simply a stage, the boards of which, so to speak, a downtrodden semi-peasantry trod, walking toward it in cheap leather huaraches and big sombreros, the olden badge of Mexico's *campesinos*. There they were ready to take their chances on illegal crossings, armed with little more than the hope of getting through and of later securing farm work. Probably such men, clad in sandals and big straw hats, would almost be welcomed by later border officials, long since faced with dealing with cosmopolitan and well-armed traffickers in drugs with whom shootouts and loss of life are commonplace in illegal transactions in which huge sums of money are involved.

Technology itself, of course, would make rents in the magic curtain. Radar nets and surveillance aircraft, high fences and wide ditches would become as much a part of the Mexican-American border as ostentatious federal buildings and armies of governmental bureaucracies and the time-consuming procedures for dealing with those who would cross the international boundary in legal fashion. It has long been that, for the border is a zone of transition, a sphere in which cultural transfusion takes place.

Borderlands themselves have long served as backgrounds for depicting social instability. They have readily been fashioned into exotic backdrops, colorful canvases for novels and tales of romanticized fiction in which hybrid characters shift easily from one culture to another. They are equally at home in both societies meeting at the magic curtain, or, at worst, they are truly at home in neither. But then bicultural lives are not for everyone. Some rebel at a duplication of virtually everything: language, customs, laws, rules and regulations, even allegiance, as well as an underlying confusion over patriotic affiliations and conscionable loyalty.

The border—the magic curtain—is the beginning of one sort of life, the ending of another. It is a hard line to walk, a difficult stage to travel. It remains a meeting ground, but often of conflict and of footloose cultural contact. For centuries the ancient borderlands have been the scene of cultural drift and change, even as they shrank and diminished into an international boundary. For decades now the magic curtain has come to symbolize imminent change. Largely it is a panorama of the working class, and of men more than of women. The scramble to earn a living makes itinerants of thousands, sometimes legal, more often not, moving out of crowded buses, trucks, railroad cars and sundry conveyances, seeing to a varied assortment of cardboard boxes and cheap straw bags, bundles wrapped in newspapers. All are the peculiar paraphernalia, the stage settings, for the magic curtain itself.

Braceros for the most part, they carry their identity in their very dress; broad-hatted in straw sombreros and always work-ready in worn denims, rough khakis, some still in faded cottons of Mexican peasant design. It is the lonely spectacle of impending separation, of field hands abruptly weaned from family and friends, and on the move for laboring in faraway places.

At times it is still to be seen: a momentary scurry, the pause for a cursory inspection at border checkpoints, the farewell in making ready to cross the great divisionary line of the two Americas—the Latin and the Anglo cultures. Going, returning, departing, arriving in a thousand different dismal depots at impoverished hours of the night, never at all certain of the longevity of their stays, the pay, the jobs, the possible brush with immigration officials, the extent of their absences shaped by the migratory work itself, the utter casualness of it all.

There is an impending sense of adventure seasoned with anxiety even to those who have accomplished such a transition before, and survived it all. The seasoned ones; they have seen it all before and lived to tell about it, even to try it again. A modest air of knowledgeability, perhaps even a few scattered phrases of English learned, a trace of the cosmopolitan hiding underlying stress and fear of the always unknown even if parts of it are familiar to those still with such states as Morelos, Chihuahua or Zacatecas written all over their faces.

Nor is it any less a vital threshold to those who daily cross the border to and from more steady employment in the dual towns and cities strung out along the nearly two-thousand-mile boundary, from Brownsville to San Diego, Matamoros to Tijuana. Workers as well as employers can still capitalize on the inequity of it all—the cheaper living conditions on one side, the higher scale of pay on the other.

Equally is it a place of would-be visitors throughout each day, travelers and tourists, students and sellers of one thing and another, sundry adventurers ever in search of that evanescent difference that is believed to exist there, somewhere en el otro lado—on the other side—on whichever part of the cultural frontier one is less familiar with. And the contraband, of course. Always the contraband in any borderland, a profitable traffic ever since one culture has come into contact with another, and the corresponding unevenness between the two. Soon or late there arises contraband in everything, in almost every endeavor, from people to products, even to thoughts, ideas, notions, frontiers of the mind vaguely formulated. Or perhaps not so vague: "*Sin fronteras*" occasionally splashed graffiti reads—No Borders, perhaps emblazoned there by some illegal boundary crosser whose journey has not been of the best.

It is not likely that such a notion will come to pass. Space takes an ever higher premium in an increasingly crowded world; it becomes institutionalized, ever more standardized, whether it is of a private or a national character. In a sense, spatial institutionalization is what borders are all about. And those who cross them learn it at firsthand. Makers of novels, tales and *corridos*—folk ballads—which deal with the border country have known it all along. It is largely what they celebrate, in story and song, from one end of the tedious border to the other and far beyond its confines as well.

Together, the corridos and the true border novels form a literature of the border country that deserves a place, a category all its own. There is an uneven quality to them all, a coarseness sometimes mixed with polish: anonymous ballads, novels of sometimes high craft and art.

It is not quite like any other category of literature, which is why it is deserving of its own special place. It is both folk art and individual artistry. At times it is rather like the epoch of the Hollywood double feature in which a B-grade movie would be shown on the same program with a film of somewhat higher quality. Long ago the motion picture industry discovered the magic curtain of the borderlands as a logical extension for horse operas with Spanish accents. There was exoticism, even a touch of glamour. It was only much later that the border itself would be rediscovered as a cinematic stage of mayhem and violence, poverty and racism, drugs and sex.

All of which could be found there, of course. Conflict arises out of all constrictions, and the world is not only a smaller place than it used to be in terms of human occupancy, it is also more readily knowable in both film and print. Fewer still are once little known areas of the world; and events such as those described in earlier folk ballads, should they happen today, might well become news stories.

Fortunately, corridos are not dead. Neither are true border novels, even though contributions to both fields are sporadic and not widely acclaimed. Or they exist farther afield, such as the numerous corridos created around the life and work of California's Cesar Chavez as founder of the United Farm Workers of America and the whole UFWA movement itself. Aspects of true border novels exist only segmentally, as part of a larger whole, such as the portion accorded the mythical settlement of Lonesome Dove in Larry

McMurtry's saga and televised film of the same name; it is simply somewhere along the Rio Grande in the sprawling riverine south of Texas. In the realm of literature of the Southwest there are others, too, which at least approach consideration as true border literature, but again only segmentally. They do not really straddle the border; neither do their characters push through the magic curtain, coping with its esoteric mysteries.

A number of such books, whether fiction or nonfiction, seldom if ever cross the magical line of demarcation between the two cultures. They remain, for the most part fully centered in either Mexico or the United States, such as some of the works of J. Frank Dobie, as in his very Texan *A Vaquero of the Brush Country* or his personalized account of his equestrian travels in northern Mexico first published as *Tongues of the Monte* and later as *The Mexico I Like.*

Still others are rather too ethnic and Indian, as in the anthropologist and novelist Oliver La Farge's *Laughing Boy* as well as in his *Cochise of Arizona (The Pipe of Peace is Broken)*. A spate of volumes, in fact, deal with the Apaches and their legendary leaders, principally Cochise and Geronimo and Mangas Coloradas, including Ross Santee's *Apache Land* and Jane Barry's *A Time in the Sun.* Some, on the other hand, are concerned entirely with reminiscences of life in the north of Mexico by expatriate English-speaking wanderers such as Dr. Ira Jefferson Bush penned in his *Gringo Doctor,* and Dan de Lara Hughes in his *South From Tombstone: A Life Story.*

While such works, and numerous others, are exemplary of borderland literature and of the American Southwest and northern Mexico in particular, they are not the true border literature that must cope with cultural identity, immigration, alienation or, in short, with most of the sundry problems imposed by the border and the magic curtain of escape which it holds forth. Taken together, border *corridos* and true border novels and tales become a literature greater than the sum of their parts. In both poetry and prose they run a gamut of emotion from the tragic to the comic, from the acceptance of obvious differences to the search for psychological realities that distinguish the peoples on either side of the magic curtain. Crossing simply underscores the basic reality of the quest for self, even to the flirtation with death to attain it.

It is in the ever-present possibility of a brush with death, that the border exists as the magic curtain of escape. Indeed, of the ultimate freedom in a Houdini-like disappearing act, or the beginning of a new life. It is that which underscores such a film as *The Getaway*, thus celebrating incipient rebirth on the other side of the cultural veil. While only the closing scenes of Peckinpah's two-hour epic chase have to do with the border, it is the crossing of it, which gives vitality and hope to the pair on the run—and with the money, yet.

Not only do Doc and Carol manage the great getaway, they do it by fleeing to the border, well prepared to pass through the magic curtain. Mexico lies only a heartbeat or so away. With the money in the bag they can purchase readily the means to that end. The former owner of the rickety vehicle—himself a seeming blend, perhaps a hybrid, of the juxtaposed cultures—remains nonplused, astonished at the apparently small fortune in U.S. dollars they insistently press upon him for the vehicle. Surely, this, too, is madness, more enchantment on the edge of the magic curtain—love and its impassioned insanity in the form of two romantically crazy Americans bound for Mexico.

How can the seller of the antiquated jalopy possibly know the recent immediacy of their long brush with death in managing the great escape? Not only have they gambled their lives and won, they have succeeded in taking along the money, too. The proximity to, the grand flirtation with, death already has taken place. Now they can drive in peace, unharmed, right through the magic curtain. Like a bad mirror, as a harbinger of grim portent, it already has been shattered. They have made it. The seedy, inconspicuous pickup will carry them to freedom and a new life on the other side. It is filmdom's classic border escape.

While Peckinpah's film, based on a novel by Jim Thompson, is not true border cinema by any means, filmmakers have indeed carved movies out of true border novels, particularly B. Traven's *The Treasure of the Sierra Madre* and Glendon Swarthout's *They Came to Cordura.* Although both, as cinematic art, lost something of the essence of their novelistic treatment as border novels, each of the approximately two-hour films manages to convey a compelling look at the vast and hard country that the border stitches together.

They Came to Cordura, a 1959 Columbia production directed by Robert Tossen, moves along too slowly for an action movie, which it purports to be. In sum, it is the story of half a dozen American soldiers and one woman trying to reach the safety of a military outpost during the time of the Mexican Revolution and the heyday of Pancho Villa, about the year 1916. While security lies in their reaching their objective, each has cause to fear, even dread, arriving there. During the course of what seems a near-endless journey, intensely personal feelings of the footloose group come into play. It is not unlike psychological counseling or group therapy in the wilderness. Even such acclaimed actors as Gary Cooper and Van Heflin, along with Rita Hayworth and Tab Hunter, are at a loss to move the action forward.

Certainly it is no match for the screenplay based on the Traven novel. The 1948 Warner Brothers film was directed by John Huston, who also executed the screenplay. Far more than most movies, the film is exceedingly faithful to the original work. Featuring Humphrey Bogart as the disturbed and ever-complaining Fred C. Dobbs, the movie casts the director's father, Walter Huston, as the elderly philosophical rascal Howard, and a young Tim Holt as the naive and easily swayed Curtin. As the luckless trio in search of the treasure, Dobbs emerges probably too strongly as a whining psychotic, but then Bogart is the star of the film. It is a powerful and very masculine movie, even if Bogart's performance almost overshadows the parable that shines through in Traven's novel.

The real treasure, the novel suggests, is never the faraway that one seeks but rather that which is always close at hand if one could but see it. Thus are greed and happenstance heavily laced with satire and irony, remarkably evinced by Alfonso Bedoya's outstanding performance as chief spokesman for a bandit group, intensifying the meeting of chaos and lawlessness. It is seemly that the two elements confront one another in the border badlands and in the long aftermath of the decade of internal fighting that had swept across Mexico in the course of revolution.

Courting death in one way or another is of course the underlying theme of both films as well as the novels on which they are based. To risk crossing through the magic curtain is to flirt with death. It is the whole game, the last chip, the final ante, and the psychological confrontation of it all is further explored in two later novels, Carlos Fuentes' *The Old Gringo* and Clifford Irving's *Tom Mix and Pancho Villa.* While the former focuses on a single death quest the latter deals with so many deaths that untimely demise is blotted into the magic curtain almost as a way of life. But, then, the magic curtain always has existed as the drape cloth, the winding sheet, of what may well be the final escape.

3

Romanticism and Reality

The movie industry of course has made capital of the borderlands and the border since early filmmakers discovered the Cisco Kid, the enduring character created by O. Henry. And while Henry's Cisco was hardly the Robin Hood sort envisioned by Hollywood, cinematic moguls proceeded to fashion a long series of films around the ongoing adventures of Cisco. As played by such Latinesque types as Cesar Romero or Duncan Renaldo, the aging Kid was the knight errant of the vast borderlands. A romantic sort of brigand, Cisco, as a kind of Jesse James, Don Juan and Don Quixote all rolled into one, was the true hybrid hero, at home on either side of the magic curtain. His territory was immense, seemingly infinite, his quests and derring-do ever pure and good. Nowhere else has the border and the borderlands ever been so continuously romanticized.

O. Henry, however, was not at all given to efforts to glorify the Cisco Kid in his short story, "The Caballero's Way," one of the nineteen brief tales that comprised his second volume of short stories published in 1907 as *Heart of the West.* But certainly the general geographical haunts of the Kid's murderous exploits were rather precisely defined. "His habitat," O. Henry informed his readers, "was anywhere between the Frio and the Rio Grande," which is, in any case, quite a sprawling section of a part of the borderlands of South Texas.

As a homicidal type his role is clear from the outset. Indeed, the Cisco Kid emerges in the opening sentence of the story as a killer who had slain six men "in more or less fair scrimmages" and "had murdered twice as many (mostly Mexicans)," the author subtly points out. In fact, Cisco seems to be the literary brother to the notorious Billy the Kid (El Chivato) because William (Billy the Kid) Bonney also was not known to keep tabs on members of minority groups he gunned down. And, of course, the Cisco Kid was El Chivato to the Spanish-speaking populace in southern Texas, just as Billy the Kid also was El Chivato to those farther west in Bonney's territory in southeastern New Mexico.

There are other parallels in the Hispanic romanticization of the realm of the magic curtain. Like Bonney, Cisco also answered to a non-Hispanic or Anglo surname—that of Goodall, a storekeeper in O. Henry's short story recalls. And, also like Bonney, who reputedly was the lover of a young Hispanic girl named Abrana García, O. Henry's Cisco Kid was the romantic partner of "a half-Mexican girl" named Tonia Perez, who resided in an impoverished condition in a lowly hut "near a little Mexican settlement at the Lone Wolf Crossing of the Frio." There she eked out a squalid existence with an aged male ancestor of uncertain kinship status, the old man herding a hundred goats and living in "a continuous drunken dream."

To say the least, Tonia received little succor from the Cisco Kid, whose way of life even kept him from being a frequent partner in romance, one of the reasons for her dalliance with another man, a Texas Ranger, in O. Henry's usual ironic twist on which the story is constructed: The Kid engineers her death because of her betrayal to him by sowing confusion in the Ranger's mind over an alleged switching of clothing between Cisco and Tonia which never took place.

Vain, cruel, utterly contemptible, the original Cisco Kid, who, O. Henry tells his readers, "was twenty-five and looked twenty," was a wanton murderer. One of his principal pastimes was "to shoot Mexicans 'to see them kick'" for he was as quick-tempered as he was quick on the draw, and was aided in eluding capture because his speckled roan horse "knew every cowpath" between San Antonio and Matamoros, opposite Brownsville, on the great border river.

If O. Henry's Cisco Kid had one saving grace, it was his reputed gallantry with women, however, that also falls by the way—"the caballero's way"—in his brutal sacrifice of the one woman who, for a time at least, had dared, or perhaps only been foolish enough, to love him. Filmdom's transformation of the Cisco Kid was almost total. The name itself and general area were essentially the sole survivors in the transformation. Moreover, O. Henry's Cisco was the quintessential loner, without any Sancho Panza-like sidekick, such as Hollywood's effervescently good-natured Chris Pin Martin, forever around to help see Cisco through thick and thin, righting wrongs and dallying with fair damsels frequently in distress, and galloping on to yet further adventures, all within the vast stage of enchantment and the bewitching vagaries occasioned by the magic curtain of the border where anything at all could happen and yet always be set aright.

The magic curtain has fluttered wherever Hispanic and Anglo customs have encountered one another along the peripheries of what was to become the Great American West. If, farther afield in olden Spanish California, the magic curtain seemed to have been raised so high as to be lost sight of as English-speaking Americans overwhelmed the Spanish-speaking populace, the transition in culture and land deals would be captured in a few stories by Bret Harte, particularly in such a tale as "Notes by

Flood and Field" in which a survey of the vast Espíritu Santo ranchlands held by Fernando Jesús María Altascar clearly will result in their reduction to the benefit of the American named Tryan. And the fading heritage is also prevalent in a few other Harte stories such as those concerning Enriquez Saltello and his sister, Consuelo, especially "The Devotion of Enriquez," "Chu Chu" and "The Right Eye of the Commander," the latter, in fact, devoting much attention to Enriquez's family heritage and his ancestor, the old comandante Antonio Hermenegildo Salvatierra.

It was out of such a nobility-ridden background as that of heraldic Spanish California that Hollywood could capitalize on the legendary Zorro in both movies and weekly serials. Zorro, the swashbuckling master swordsman and savior of the poor, was olden California's aristocratic Robin Hood, black-masked and clad in black from head to toe. Black, too, were the further tools of his trade: his faithful stallion and punishing whip. Thus with foil and lash, the inimitable Fox was ever ready to right all wrongs, and in his wake slash out his famous Z imprint, the mark of Zorro. But though the uncanny Fox seemed to be everywhere, when pursued he was nowhere. At once Zorro disappeared into his shadow self—effete scion of nobility and pillar of the status quo, the role customarily played by veteran Anglo-American actors Robert Livingstone and Reed Hadley. Not until 1998, half a century later, would Zorro dash back to glory with Antonio Banderas wearing *The Mask of Zorro.*

But the stage for the magic curtain was, and remains, immense. America's golden-voiced singing cowboy Gene Autry passed through the magic curtain in both film and song from time to time in moderately memorable efforts such as *Mexicali Rose* and *South of the Border (Down Mexico Way)* even as later Mexico's answer to Autry, Miguel Aceves Mejía, the little man with the big voice, did much the same sort of thing. And eventually Mexican filmmakers, too, would confront the magic curtain with such fare as *Otro Lado del Puente (The Other Side of the Bridge)* and *La*

Muerte Cruza el Río Bravo (Death Crosses the Rio Grande), but most especially with the emotionally charged classic *El Norte (The North)*.

Nor, since the Cisco Kid film exploits of the 1930s and early '40s would it ever again be so romanticized. But the border itself would figure prominently in other movies, to the point of making certain that the very word was used in some way in the cinematic title. Where western romanticism had triumphed before, now a grim and oftentimes seedy reality was to be the motif.

Such was the case in the 1933 movie *Bordertown,* a sexually intense drama built on a love triangle and based on a novel by Carroll Graham. Whisking away the magic curtain to provide a tawdry if exotic backdrop, the one hour and forty minutes of cinematic escape directed by Archie Mayo revolve around Paul Muni as a gone-to-seed lawyer who has foolishly got himself involved with Bette Davis as the bored wife of jowly, three-chinned Eugene Pallette in the role of the local businessman.

Again, in 1949, a semidocumentary presentation of sorts was unveiled as *Border Incident,* featuring Ricardo Montalban and George Murphy. A shabbily sinister tale about illegal immigrants and murder, the ninety-two-minute film directed by Anthony Mann is a reasonably well-made drama. Although Montalban seems perhaps a bit too suave for his role as immigration officer used as decoy to break up a large market in what in effect is virtually slave trading, attention is called to the sad plight of illegals and those who prey upon them. But there is a degree of success, in the film at any rate, in coping with the problem of unlawful crossings and exploitation of those caught in the folds of the magic curtain.

Much of the same sort of tale of exploitation was also hatched in *Borderline,* a 1950 cinema offering starring Fred MacMurray and Claire Trevor that shifted the current of criminality from contraband in humans to that in narcotics. With drug smugglers working the border area below Los Angeles, the somewhat farcical melodrama has Trevor in the role of policewoman packed off to get the goods on the culprits.

Yet, if border realism was to run only a brief course, the border itself was still a drawing card. Four years later the time seemed ripe for a border historical romance, and one was mustered for the purpose. *Border River,* a 1954 swashbuckler, went back to the days of the Civil War for its story line. Featuring Yvonne De Carlo and Joel McCrea, along with Pedro Armendariz and Howard Petrie, the eighty-minute film seems long on action, short on dramatic content. But, in keeping with its historical perspective, the movie, directed by George Sherman, was free to draw on a variety of colorful characters in the course of dispatching McCrea, as a Confederate officer, down to Mexico to purchase arms for the South's already lost cause.

Border River, though, was really outside the pale of what already had become an increasingly seedy if not sinister view of the international boundary and its recurrent turmoil, cultural conflict and tragedy. Indeed, those would become mundane as more alien troublespots entered the national limelight, stealing a march on the now-jaded exoticism once provided by the magic curtain and its allure of escape.

Only after thirty years was it time for yet another crusty border incident from filmdom, this one in 1980 also entitled *Borderline* and starring Charles Bronson as his usual wooden self. The dour Bronson, in the film directed by Gerrold Freeman, is cast as a Border Patrol officer on the trail of a murderer roaming the border area—again, as in the 1950 movie, along the California sector. Action largely stands in for both acting and interpretation in the ninety-seven-minute movie.

Getting even more into the heart of the matter two years later was the film simply called *The Border,* director Tony Richardson's 1982 cinematic presentation of general border wickedness. The one-hour-and-forty-seven-minute movie features Jack Nicholson as the central protagonist, along with Harvey Keitel, Valerie

Perrine, Warren Oates, Elpidia Carrillo and Shannon Wilcox. Nicholson is the hero, trying to remain honest while corruption among border officials runs rampant. So, too, does the ongoing exploitation of Mexican illegals, although an overview of moral uprightness is by and large sacrificed for a fast-paced and typically action-filled film.

As the magic curtain of escape, however, the drama goes on. If it cannot be done in modern realism, there is always the historical and legendary trappings of the past, whether book or film, that can be launched every few years. Thus, following on the heels of *The Getaway* was the film *Goin' South* (1978) in which horse thief Henry Moon (Jack Nicholson) outrides a posse across the Rio Grande only to be brought back across the river to be hanged. A little-known statute saves him from the gallows: If a woman speaks up for him to become her husband, the condemned man goes free. One does: Mary Steenburgen, in the role of Julia, a woman working a gold mine nearby the mythical border town and who is desperately in need of a strong back to help her exploit the treasure.

While the lightweight spoof is less than memorable, after a number of pitfalls in the trial marriage-mining arrangement, the two learn to trust if not genuinely love one another after a rich vein of gold is found. Ultimately Henry persuades Julia to strike out for the country he loves, Mexico. (Actually, they already are there—the movie was filmed in the state of Durango.) The horse, laden with their gold, shambles toward what seemingly is south, and the legendary border, as the two, Henry and Julia, now obviously united as one in mutual caring and wealth, follow along on foot.

So the border lives, realistically as well as fictionally. If at times it seems little more than an international zone of stagnation and corruption, it is also one of challenge and hope—both sides of it. People still escape to either side of it, romantics as well as realists, dreamers as well as sellers of a dream. The border remains the magic curtain—Alice's Looking Glass—through which one passes into something else, into a different world, even though it now is a much more precise and measured one, no longer little-known territory about which much could be recounted and remembered, even if it was not true.

Seemingly, then, there is no longer much glamour to be found in the grim reality, the sordid conditions of a life expressed in such later films dealing with the border. It becomes rather a painful place, a clime of continuing transience, even for those of settled roots who are brushed all the while by a nomadic presence, by those who would cross the magic curtain as well as those who would profit from their doing so.

In such a view no one now rides off into the sunset across the enchanted realm and into a new life, as in *The Getaway.* Escape itself, even unto death, is stymied. The game of crossing becomes more intense, the number of players increases; so do the bureaucracies watching over them. The goal itself gets to be more elusive, more fraught with peril.

Many, perhaps most, seem as luckless as Dobbs, the ill-fated plunderer of *The Treasure of the Sierra Madre,* trying to re-enter the realm of the magic curtain. But, burdened with his fortune in gold, Dobbs himself no longer can find his way back. Not rationally, at any rate. He already has succumbed to the irreality from which he would escape, trapped, as it were, by the very madness that has overtaken him on the other side of the magic curtain. Few indeed are those who can pass through the curtain, then re-emerge wholly as once they were on the curtain's other side.

The magic curtain is transformation itself, the embodiment of change. It is a storied place that alters all who pass through it in one form or another. And it remains the visionary's kingdom of the eternal quest for whatever goal the would-be-seeker searches; perhaps, unfortunately, it is no more real than the vision itself or the intensity of it. It changes endlessly and constantly, even as the search itself is transformed. The magic alone survives, is real, the sole constant in its inconstancy. And the much-romanticized realm is seen to be as transparent as the curtain itself and the enchantment it is believed to convey.

More abreast of the changing times is the no-frills, cut-to-the-chase action film *El Mariachi.* By the 1990s drugs and assault weapons have invaded the boundary area, along with the endless cycle of workers thrown out of work by technological innovations. In this case it's a lone *mariachi* guitar player losing out to electronic synthesizers that sound like full *mariachi* bands. Synthesizers don't, of course, but quality is constantly sacrificed for quantity in the new age of mass culture cost cutting.

Further in keeping with the anonymity of the mass culture age is the nameless protagonist, the wandering solitary guitarist, appropriately clad in funereal black. So, too, is his unlikely nemesis, newly sprung from the culture of big money, drugs and violence. Here is another black-clad figure with a guitar case; however, this one is a killer with a guitar case full of semi-automatic assault weapons, and now being hunted down by the hirelings of a drug lord.

It's all a fast-paced case of mistaken identity. *El Mariachi* is full of border town shootouts, whizzing bullets, and rampant thrills of an inexpensive nature—the 1992 movie was made at a reported cost of $7,000 by Robert Rodriguez, a then twenty-four-year-old Texan. Rodriguez himself thus demonstrates yet another aspect of the endless technological revolution—the rise of the independent filmmaker with the handcrafted movie who doesn't need a Hollywood studio for his handiwork.

The border itself will serve nicely as a unique but sufficiently grimy backdrop; and with the dialogue in Spanish and an English narration, it's a bicultural sort of achievement. The new technologies and their attendant styles of life seem altogether settled in, all of a piece with the hero anonymous, worker displacement, and a lawlessness boldly taken into the streets. Modish relevance prevails. Intrusion into the magic curtain is stunningly complete.

The sadder and sobering fact, however, is the acceptance of the drug subculture with its attendant violence and nonchalant disregard for human life as established fait accompli. It is simply the way things are—one of the new hazards of life to be reckoned with, as much a part of the incipient twenty-first century as computerization and cloning, corporate arrogance, genetic engineering, behavioral science. Anything is a candidate for commodification; incivility flourishes, and civil disobedience is recycled as civil contempt.

Films such as *El Mariachi* and *Desperado*, Rodriguez's rip-off redoing *El Mariachi* three years later, reflect the currency of sleazy reality. Life in the streets is perilous; parking lots are a no man's land that can erupt into battle zones. In the ever proliferating car culture the vehicle itself is a licensed weapon. The only thing we now have to fear is each other.

By the turn of the century, the border in film had come full circle with two movies, *Traffic* and *All the Pretty Horses*, appearing in theaters almost back to back. While *Traffic* epitomizes the drug-ridden now, *All the Pretty Horses* glamorizes the romantic-laden then. *All the Pretty Horses* is a quasi-modern horse opera with Mexican accessories. Two young cowboy types set out to gallop across the border into Mexico. Trailed early on by a young boy who seeks to join them, the men reluctantly permit him to ride along. Theirs is a bad decision. Rash actions of the impetuous boy, a volatile presence waiting to erupt, eventually cause his death and very nearly cost the lives of his two companions.

Preposterous as it seems, the two young men find work as horsebreakers for a powerful hacendado. And the hacendado, it so happens, has a nubile and headstrong daughter. Quite a horsewoman herself, she soon is the lover of one of the foreigners.

Director Billy Bob Thornton's movie is faithful to the general plot of Cormac McCarthy's novel of the same name, but the film is too brief to convey the leisurely time frame of the adventure. Nor can the dialogue capture the subtle nuances of McCarthy's sometimes pensive prose, high-flown language and fancy manner of storytelling. Jobs breaking horses do not last; nor does passion, particularly between so ill-matched a pair as an itinerant ranch hand and an aristocratic hacienda heiress. On film, it all seems a bit like spring fling south of the border, but at a time when the border still was curtained in mystery and the satisfying distinction of difference.

With the arrival of *Traffic,* the border became the personification of evil. Drugs and the drug war are the protagonists, and the border is the seedy star of narcotrafficking whose seductive horrors invade all walks of life on either side of the boundary. Here at last, it would seem, is a film that has got it all down pat, a movie that shows the boundary for what it is. Here is the true borderless world wherein corruption is boundless and moral degradation is infinite, as bottomless as the wages of sin.

So much money is involved in the drug war business that drugs are like an international currency, the bargaining chip of clandestine power politics. No longer can one distinguish the good guys from the bad. The one side beds down with the other. There are no strange bedfellows in Steven Soderbergh's interweaving of a trio of stories about the war on drugs: cops versus corruption in ambiguous drug busts; a drug czar whose teenage daughter is an addict; and an unscrupulous wife trying to hang on to an illicit fortune following the arrest of her drug-lord husband.

At last the border is a *Traffic* guerrilla war zone, a slag heap of atrocities, a world of sleaze in which nothing is what it seems to be—or, then again, maybe it is. In any case, it is as depraved on one side as the other. Interminable lines of traffic radiate heat waves undulating in the desert around San Diego and Tijuana. There is no magic curtain here through which to pass, only grim reality. The curtain is gone, collapsed under the sprawling sameness of a mass culture that is egalitarian in its greed, hedonism, amorality, and unlimited violence accomplished with high-tech proficiency.

Materialism strides forth bolder than ever; greed is unassailable. An overabundance of people means there are simply more suckers to exploit. Drug lords and dope peddlers are merely entrepreneurs who have to protect their markets more vigorously than do other sorts of business people. But it's okay—beneath the amoral exterior lies the heart of a modern-day Robin Hood. Smuggling, dealing in contraband, servicing a black market economy is no longer penny-ante stuff, it's big business, and it's big bucks.

The enemy is government itself, and thus the drug dealer can emerge as even more of a hero, the champion contender against an implacable foe. Big money and fast living are as potent as the drugs, the purveyors of which can be glamorized in latter-day corridos that are no longer simply folkloric ballads, and the drug dealer, the powerful *traficante*, has become the folk hero.

Corridos are still created, and so is true border fiction, even if both have not quite the aura of exoticism they once had. The world has changed too much for that. The once unknown has become the familiar; the once little known and little recognized the commonplace. Uncharted areas for the makers of ballads, novels, movies have receded. One can scarcely venture into any realm where someone has not gone before.

The world is a less fabled place. And the lengthy, narrow world of the border is now a more prosaic one. Within its confines a grimmer sense of reality prevails, particularly for the producers of corridos, films, stories that purport to convey some essence of so distinctive a sphere of life in an increasingly high-tech universe.

Thus the body of works discussed herein are exemplary rather than comprehensive. They are representative in pointing the way to that once-fabled frontier as a most unusual boundary, a curtained realm of enchantment, as it were, through which from either side one passed into a clime of foreign adventures. Passing through so magical a curtain betokened immediate escapades both realistic and idyllic, new cultural identities, changes in habits of thought, in the way of viewing others as well as one's own self.

Inevitably perhaps, it cloaked a realm of romance. It is a realm now for the most part covered over by a globalization grown more standardized at every turn, a globalization of products whose uniformity may erase even the individuality of once-unique border areas. Perhaps only in verse and prose can the border live on as the magic curtain of escape and transformation of individual lives.

And all the while the border itself has changed, has, as the economic phrase states, turned the corner, and come of age. No longer is it rustic, remote, parochial. Instead, urbanity has settled in, even a kind of sleazy glamour associated with Mafia toughness, hard as a diamond and just as brilliant as such a gem in the superficial sophistication that has transformed the border into a harsher reality. The magic has faded somewhat; the curtain grown more tawdry with age—some of its once magical secrets let out of the bag as people learn more about one another, including some things they may not like. Friction, of course, is inevitable in human relationships; and with the rise in populations and their attendant pressures the incidence for such friction increases.

So, too, does the market and the traffic in contraband increase—suppliers of hard drugs simply catering to what is called "the American disease." Seen in that light, they are merely merchants battling an age-old nemesis, the United States in its omnivorous role as the Colossus of the North. The siren song of illegal crossings and of contraband has a different cast of characters and a different theme. The stakes are higher, and the payoff frequently an early death. It is a balladry of the era of the *narcotraficante* in a borderland of increasing surveillance utilizing high-tech instruments that might be employed in any military operation.

The once-magic curtain has become rather a lantern show of despair. Life is cheapened even as a commercial kind of cosmopolitanism gains sway along the border that becomes more heavily trafficked, more populated, more politicized. In a new age a new curtain might yet descend upon it. If so, it will not be the magic curtain of yore.

That is as it should be, of course; if a curtain rises, it also falls, ready to rise anew. Ever since the great cession of Mexican territory and the establishing of the border, a whimsical notion has prevailed that the United States should force Mexico to take back the whole area. In whimsy there is an element of truth; but wherever the border is, there too is the looking glass with which to reflect on individual differences.

Part Two:

The Poetry

4

Rhymes for Rampant Change

The older borderland ballads—or corridos as they are called in Spanish—necessarily derive from the area first settled by Spanish colonists along the lower reaches of the Rio Grande, from the Great River's mouth in the Gulf of Mexico upstream as far as the twin cities of Laredo and Nuevo Laredo. Over the long years, as the far-flung provinces of New Spain ultimately became Mexico, and later as large areas of Mexico became parts of the United States, conflict and strife flowed all along the newly determined border.

Borderland residents, individuals to the core, whether heroes or antiheroes, were often given to taking matters into their own hands. Not infrequently they found themselves in conflict with existing regimes on both sides of the long boundary, at times seeking to effect political coups for which there existed only minimal popular support. In short, many such men seemed marked from the outset for noble failure.

Numerous corridos celebrate incidents befalling those running afoul of the law—from bandits to smugglers, large landholders with a taste for yet more landed acquisitions, Texas Rangers and, inevitably, cattle dealers and rustlers (who often were one and the same). Still others recount the derring-do of such once well-known border figures as Juan Cortina (the "Red Robber of the Rio Grande") and Catarino Garza, dreamers of lost causes and proponents of independent border republics who were perhaps ahead of their time in hosting allegiance neither to Mexico nor to the United States.

But the corridos of the border country relate much more than mere tales of revolt, banditry and overtures to a sort of hybrid patriotism born of fomenting new empires. The borderland ballads are the voice of a people coming to feel themselves hemmed in, contained, pushed in one way or another from both sides of the international boundary. The once-magic curtain falls; once vacuous and open space becomes steadily institutionalized, standardized.

Hero or antihero becomes caught up within the framework of an ongoing rivalry from which there is seemingly no way out and thus emerges as either an outlaw with slightly elevated motives or merely a motivated brigand with no elevated aims at all. Both are the result of swift and compelling change in the internationalized order; along the border, change is so rampant that the most stable life becomes little more than that of continuing conflicts.

The boundary itself becomes an arbiter of moral codes, the dispassionate evaluator of which action is that of the patriotic revolutionary and which only that of the plunderer motivated by self-interest. The magic of the border itself draws the fine distinction between what might be considered reasonable commercial endeavor on the one hand and simply smuggling and black marketing on the other. Even honest labor and the route to gainful employment become an area of illegal activity when governed by the economics of the border, or the exploitation of the already exploited.

Corridos of the borderlands faithfully reflect those aspects particularly as the boundary becomes a settled institution, entrenches itself as an economic as well as a political force in daily life. It becomes the grist of the corridos, just as it becomes the duty of the ballad makers to recite those things which have come to pass. The protagonists—*gringos, fuereños, pochos*—are thus, if not immortalized, then at least awarded their proper roles in the hybrid cultural transformation that has shaped the border populaces both to the north and south of the once-magic curtain of escape.

The people south of the international boundary have long been a ballad-making public. Such ballads, or corridos as they are known in Mexico, are not only a vital part of life beyond the magic curtain, they also have played a significant role wherever Mexicans and Mexican Americans have gathered. And while corridos may be simply recited or read, they are designed to be sung to the accompaniment of the guitar, so long the favored instrument of transient minstrels and troubadours.

After centuries of existence as one of the most popular of poetic forms in the public domain, corridos, necessarily perhaps, have become highly stylized, simplistic even; unabashedly they are no more than what they purport to be—rhyming couplets or quatrains that unfold some tale, episode, anecdote or virtually any event considered worth calling to attention, either for pleasure or to convey some moral precept. Translated, they become, much like any other creation, subject to transplant shock, losing their rough brilliance in foreign linguistic soil.

A few—not many—of the corridos of Mexico have risen above their normally mundane level; a handful have attained the unlikely status of symbolizing some national event, a feat little less than remarkable in a nation noted for its regional differences.

La Cucaracha has indeed become truly international. For many it is not only the primal ballad of the Mexican Revolution, it is Mexico itself. Other Revolutionary ballads of renown, *Adelita* or *La Valentina,* do not rise to such heights. Indeed, the bulk of corridos are largely provincial and far less imbued with the patina of grand events.

Taken as a whole, such ballads convey a part of the history of the great social and political revolt even while at the same time they celebrate the diverse cultural backgrounds of the republic. Mexico has long had its extensive regional differences, which have persisted even under the leveling of social orders under pervasive technological change.

On a broader scale, it has its very different east and west coasts, its own great north and south, each quite dissimilar, not only geographically but culturally and demographically. An Emiliano Zapata of the south can never be quite the same as a Pancho Villa of the north, and much of what is related in corridos attuned to Revolutionary unity is still regionalistic, even parochial.

As a poetic form, the corrido is readily traced back to Spain and the short lyrical epic poems known as romances, which, by the time of the Castillians' great moment on the world stage, the Golden Age of the sixteenth century, had become quite a significant part of what was to emerge as Spanish culture. By then they were a part of the heritage of the peoples of the Iberian peninsula, but the stories and sentiments embedded in the romances were not destined for enduring success in the New World. Not only did they deal with incidents and figures peculiarly Castillian, they were also Moorish in scope as well. Indeed, they had much to say about counts and kings of an alien order and they reached across seven hundred years of religious conflict between Christians and Muslims in the land that had become Spain.

Romanceros, creators of such lyrics, delighted in embroidering themes of treachery and tragedy, seduction and love, the cultural as well as the color line between the dark-skinned Islamic Moors, the Saracenic invaders of Spain and their descendants who were to remain there for seven centuries, and the fairer Christian Iberians. Idealized poetic epics, they were carved from that sphere wherein history and legend intermingle to become one.

The theme of religious and cultural conflict between the followers of Mohammed and those of Christ in fact runs through much of the romance literature. It was carried forward by later writers, such as Lope de Vega, the eminent and prolific playwright of the sixteenth century, in his *Romance de Zaide:*

—Mira, Zaide, que te aviso
que no pases por mi calle
ni hables con mis mujeres
ni con mis cautivos trates . . .

Confieso que eres valiente,
que rajas, hiendes y partes
y que has muerto más cristianos
que gotas tienes de sangre. . . .

"Look, Zaide, let me warn thee
That thou not pass through my street,
Neither speak with my women
Nor with my captives treat . . .

I admit thou art brave
Thou canst slash and stab and club,
And thou hast slain more Christians
Than thou hast drops of blood. . . ."

More commonplace events were worthy topics of anonymous romances also, particularly if they fueled the ever-smoldering strife between the two groups. A further example is provided in the historic ballad exemplifying the volatile relations as seen in the kidnapping of three young Christian girls, all sisters, who had strayed into Moorish or Morisco territory, as depicted in the anonymous *Las tres cautivas (The Three Captives)*:

En el campo moro
entre las olivas,

allí cautivaron
tres niñas perdidas;
el pícaro moro
que las cautivó
a la reina mora
se las entregó. . . .

On Moorish land,
Among the olive trees,
There three lost maidens
They did seize;
The knavish Moor
Who captured them
To the Moorish queen
Did surrender them. . . .

A certain majesty and grandeur, however, winds through most of the medieval romances. Accounts taken from happenings memorializing numerous figures of the nobility were ready to hand. They ranged from such vaunted exploits as those of the heroic Count Fernán González and Conde (Count) Arnaldos to the renowned saga of El Cid. Or they recounted the infamous slaughter of the seven young Lara brothers as the result of treachery in their assumed "wicked" marriages in an ongoing blood feud as told in the *Romance de los siete infantes de Lara* or celebrated the noble reign of Alfonso el sabio (Alfonso the Wise, king of León and Castille, 1252-84).

Some of the bolder romanceros might indeed wax political, imparting counsel to their rulers, such as that given Sancho Ordóñez of the kingdom of León:

—Rey don Sancho, rey don Sancho
no digas que no te aviso,
que de dentro de Zamora
un alevoso ha salido. . . !—

"King sire Sancho, King sire Sancho,
Do not sayest I do not thee warn,
That out of the city of Zamora
Comes treachery to do thee harm. . . !"

It goes almost without saying then that in the New World many of the stories, even the sentiments, embedded in the old romances were not destined to be transplanted, although certainly the basic poetic form was to endure. There are ballads in print in Mexico from the time of the conquest by the Spaniards in the sixteenth century, however the bulk of Mexican corridos date from the 1800s. Thus, while they are well grounded in the past, they are continuing fragments of the national epic, created usually by a folk, or unlettered, people.

Corridos, though—it bears repeating—were not so much written as they were recited or sung, and stored in the heart as well as in the head. They are personalized moments from the past. And like the sentiment expressed in one of the ancient anonymous romances, one sang one's song only to those who followed the singer: "Yo no digo mi canción, sino a quien conmigo va."

Not only does it become the object of corridos to foster a pride in regional consciousness and indeed to exalt those insular features that make the community distinctive, it also becomes the mission of the ballads to pay homage to their particular audience. Perhaps in no better way is this done than in paying tribute to their women.

Because the making of corridos has been properly the province of men, it has fallen to balladeers to celebrate—sometimes with faint scorn—the women of the regions and communities of which they sing. One of the more salient examples may be seen in the ballad, *La Iguana,* from the Mexican-American border state of Sonora. First taken to task, in a manner of praising with faint damns, are the young women of Nacozari, one of the state's principal towns:

Las muchachas de Nacozari
son altas y delgaditas;
pero son mas pedigüeñas
que las ánimas banditas.

The girls of Nacozari
Are lissomly tall and slight,
But they beggar for more attention
Than the vesper bells at night.

The battle of the sexes, of course, is traditionally part of the general theme and baggage of corridos. And, rather traditionally, too, if a compliment is rendered on the one hand, then with the other it is taken away. A leavening process, so to speak, is the result.

But such flowery judgments must be weighed against something else, some other form of comparison inveighing against utter provinciality. Thus, as if to display what might be termed a cosmopolitan regionality, the balancing out of feminine wiles in *La Iguana* is continued. The focus turns to another Sonoran city, that of Navojoa:

Las chicas de Navojoa
pasan la vida en la plaza,
mirando por todas partes,
por ver si un marido pasa.

The girls of Navojoa
Spend all their lives on the square
Surveying the scene about them,
In search of a husband to snare.

While sexism is one of the primal themes of popular treatment, it is rather the ballads that commemorate some epic event or a quasi-political figure of renown that are capable of transcending their own regionality and achieving a much broader appeal. Some of those, such as the ones stemming from the chaotic days of the Revolution, endure not only because of their celebration of the drama common to the national heritage, but also because of some of the memorable melodies on which the themes are strung. In that, they rise above the recitations of individual boasting or personalized recollections.

In those, moralistic prescripts are conveyed only infrequently, but when they are, the ground is laid early on for such preachments. A typical opening for the recitation of a woeful example of errant behavior is provided in that which the prodigal son is about to unfold in the *Corrido del hijo pródigo:*

> *Señores, vengo a contarles*
> *una triste narración,*
> *de lo que sufre hoy en día*
> *por no tener reflexión.*
>
> Gentlemen, I've come here to tell you
> A truly sorrowful tale,
> Over which I today still suffer
> For not having considered too well.

Prodigality, the sexist battle, the penalties of flirtatious behavior, the marital quest, all are grist for the mills of balladeering, of course. And at times a corrido may relate some happening so characteristic, so typical of life everywhere that it, the event itself, becomes a handy reference to the consequences of such conduct.

Thus, for example, in the *Corrido de Rosa,* the warning administered at the outset typically conveys the aura of prospective fear, the universal notion of "I told you so" that seems bound to happen. Disregarding her mother's counsel, Rosa herself sets the stage for what might be the seemingly inevitable:

Su mamá se lo decía:
Rosa, esta noche no sales.
Mamá, no tengo la culpa
que a mí me gusten los bailes.

Her mother kept on telling her,
Rose, please don't go out tonight.
Mama, it isn't my fault that
To me dances are such a delight.

But while the very personal, the familial, is treated in such a ballad as the *Corrido de Rosa,* others are sufficiently broad in scope as to deal with social history itself, with things of the moment as well as with change itself. A stunning example is apparent in the ballad celebrating the birth of electric power lighting in *La luz eléctrica.* Even more to the point is the mark of progress heralded in the coming of streetcars in *Los trenes eléctricos:*

Es una invención magnífica
la que se mira hoy en México
y que sorprende muchísimo
a toda la capital.

'Tis a magnificent invention
That today in the capital is viewed,
Through the whole of Mexico City
It astonishes the multitude.

Variations on the general themes of the corridos are virtually inexhaustible; they are, after all, not only of the people but also by and for the people. Moreover, with the highly rhythmic sense for which the Spanish language is wondrously fitted, the corridos, the true offspring of the medieval romances, relate with a straightforward simplicity the seemingly surface happenings that, for the most part, require little embellishment in order to convey the underlying psychology and course of action of which the brief stories speak.

It is indeed in that very simplicity that the corrido has its reason for being, its lifeblood, and in its rudimentary, even simplistic, poetic form lies its greatness as well as its continuing folk-like appeal. And although the stanzas may vary, from four to six, even eight lines, the most common by far remain the quatrains, and especially those that contain eight syllables to the line.

As balladeers, the people of north Mexico, and the descendants of those whose lives have been changed if not directly shaped by the Mexican-American border, have had no less a role than others thoughout the republic in creating corridos that depict their own special history and experience. But the corridos of the north country—of the border—do differ from the general run in that the contact of so many corrido protagonists has so often been with Americans, as well as with certain episodes and events of the United States experience in general.

They are, then, the living history of the strife and conflict flowing always over the international boundary, from one side to the other, across the magic curtain of escape, the invisible—at times only imaginary—line of change. As long as ballad makers, *copleros*, endure in the border country, such will be the case.

5

The Arbiter of Moral Codes

Corridos of the border country are not particularly dedicated simply to commemorating legendary figures and questionable wrongdoers and, by virtue of that, thus depicting by precept and example some idealized code of conduct. They are too close to actual events to have to resort to total fabrication and the manufacture of presumed ideals. Life as celebrated in corridos, is sufficiently picaresque that there is little need for ballad makers to have to fictionalize and make up everything.

In mere daily existence there is no end of subject matter; every person has at least one story probably worth telling—if not, it can be embellished a bit. All is material for a balladeer. Perhaps the best face can be put on whatever has happened that is within the public domain or the storied memories of but a few. But perhaps it cannot; corridos are rather nondiscriminatory within the context of their own cultural milieu.

A case in point is the *Corrido de los Pronunciados (Ballad of the Insurrectionists)*, which depicts a well-intentioned but ignominious border incident in perhaps the best light possible.

Insurrection is ever a risky undertaking, and armed interventionists emanating from foreign soil are doubly vulnerable.

Even as a cause célèbre, the insurrectionist undertaking is a lost cause from the start. Rafael Ramírez, a rancher in south Texas, had contributed funds for backing armed intervention against the regime of Porfirio Díaz, following the lead of the revolutionary Catarino Garza and his pronouncement condemning the dictator. Under the ostensible leadership of yet another extraterritorial proponent, Darío Hernández, approximately fifty men had been assembled with the goal of invading the Mexican republic on its northern border and overthrowing the benevolent dictator in faraway Mexico City. Before any well-conceived plan of action could be effected, however, Ramírez already had withdrawn his support in the dubious venture. Consequently, what had at best been little more than a filibustering expedition from the start had been reduced to but a contingent of armed adventurers positioned at the threshold of the international boundary and bent on creating what diplomats in their cautious phraseology would term a border incident. Notwithstanding the loss of their financial backer, the interventionist force proceeded with their commitment, crossing the international river near the small settlement of San Ignacio, some fifty miles downstream from Laredo.

From there they continued deeper into Mexico, eventually laying siege to the Tortillas ranch. The Tortillas was situated in the adjacent border state of Tamaulipas, which for decades had been a hotbed of international strife, border contentiousness and a number of pronouncements, those revolutionary proclamations ever dear to the politicized hearts of Mexicans.

In typical fashion of corridos tribute is paid to Garza. Díaz is soundly renounced, and Hernández and his hapless followers nonetheless manage to acquit themselves quite well. The entire incident is disposed of in the thirteen quatrains of the historic corrido.

Corrido de los Pronunciados

El día diez de diciembre
¡Qué día tan señalado!
En el rancho de Las Tortillas
Siete muertos han causado.

Cuando pasaron el río
Cantando varias canciones,
Gritaban los Pronunciados,
—Vamos buscando ladrones.—

El domingo en la mañana
Como por el camposanto,
Unos hombres a caballo,
Se vió un tanto cuanto.

Partieron en la violencia
Que parecía que volaban,
—¡Viva Catarino Garza!—
A grito abierto gritaban.

Gritaba el jefe Salinas:
—Hoy tienen que sobrar liachos,
Arrímense a los primeros,
Echen pie a tierra, muchachos.

La primera a la derecha,
La segunda por el centro,
La tercera por la izquierda,
Muchachos, todos adentro.—

El estruendo de la guardia
Se oyó resonar muy feo,

No más vieron el cuartel,
Y se formó el tiroteo.

Gritaban los Pronunciados:
—¡Ríndanse, hijos de un cuerno!—
—¡No, no rendimos!—decían.
—¡Viva el Supremo Gobierno!—

Ese José Besarrubia
Muy mal herido quedó,
Y entre poquitos momentos
Del mundo se separó.

El capitán Darío Hernández
Al asistente tumbó,
Por interés del sombrero,
Cinco balazos le dió.

Gritaba un Pronunciado
A orillas de una barranca:
—¡Alto el fuego, compañeros,
Se vió una bandera blanca!—

Se hicieron de los caballos
De carabinas y sillas,
Gritaban los Pronunciados,
—¡Esto lo cargan a Díaz!

Gritaban los Pronunciados
Con demasiado valor:
—Esto lo cargan a Díaz,
Si, al cabo, es buen pagador.—

Ballad of the Insurrectionists

That day, the tenth of December,
Oh, what a remarkable date!
On the ranch of Las Tortillas,
Seven met death as their fate.

Soon after crossing the river,
Singing various melodies,
Boldly shouted the Rebels,
"Let's go looking for Díaz's thieves!"

Then, on the morning of Sunday,
With everything quiet as a tomb,
Mounted men, off in the distance,
Riding furiously, there in the gloom.

Swiftly they made way for a fracas,
So quickly it seemed they had flown;
"Long live Catarino Garza!"
They shouted in thundering tone.

Cried out Commander Salinas:
"Today they'll get more than they want!
Move in, boys! Close up the lead troops!
And hit the ground hard, you up front!

"Off to the right there, the first file!
Second one, down through the heart!
Away to the left, now, the third file!
Come on, boys, let's all do our part!"

The din of the Federal troopers
Resounded gravely there in the quiet,
No sooner were seen the troopers
Than the skirmish broke out in a riot.

Boldly shouted the Rebels:
"Give up, you cuckolds of Díaz the fool!"
"We'll never give up," they shouted.
"Long live the Porfirian rule!"

Good old José Besarrubia
Got a bad wound where he stood,
And in but a very few moments
Had departed from this world for good.

Rebel Captain Darío Hernández,
When a certain hat captured his eye,
Knocked off the chief subaltern,
With five bullets which he let fly.

Then shouted one of the Rebels
From the banks of a nearby ravine,
"Hold off your fire there, compatriots,
For a white flag has now just been seen."

Then they made off with the rifles,
As well as the saddles and mounts,
And boldly the Rebels all shouted,
"Just charge these to Díaz's accounts!"

Still once more they shouted,
More boldly they had their last say,
"Just charge these to President Díaz!
He's the best in the world to pay!"

The *Corrido de los Pronunciados* or *Ballad of the Insurrectionists* is fairly illustrative of several revolutionary inspired efforts aimed at ousting various political regimes over the years. And, like the *Pronunciados,* the origins of many such corridos owe their birth, in effect, to the international boundary, the magic-curtained atmosphere of the borderlands in which the Mexican and American cultures meet.

But many, too, again like the *Pronunciados,* were destined to be shorn of their idealism and espoused political causes early on. Quite rapidly they could degenerate into mere bands of mercenaries and adventurers who easily transformed a political ideal into little more than a foray for personal gain and aggrandizement simply through inflicting havoc on the status quo and the general populace at large. Frequently indeed they were precisely that—raiding parties bent on plunder and not at all averse to bending the international boundary to their own advantage.

Even so, the corridos are generally faithful in their depictions, making proper distinctions between mere banditry on the one hand and "pronouncements" in support of particular political persuasions on the other. Nor are they generally embroidered beyond the usual liberties taken with poetic license, and the recounting of events in a sufficiently folklike manner.

Border raiding, of course, was common on both sides of the Great River that provided a mantle of escape, a sort of territorial standard, the crossing of which seemingly provided a safe haven. While all were economically inspired in essence, some were perhaps more retaliatory than others.

One of the last such rather large border raids, for example, took place in August 1916, when a party of Mexicans crossed the Rio Grande—Río Bravo—about midway between the towns of Matamoros and Reynosa along the lower reaches of the river. A Texas Ranger, however, had witnessed the movement of the group into United States territory and immediately forwarded a report of the crossing to a company of Rangers at Brownsville, the comparable American twin city of Mexico's Matamoros.

Two days later a number of the Mexican force lost their lives in a running gun battle with the Ranger contingent when they were barely a mile away from the protection, more imaginary than real, of the international river boundary. During the intervening couple of days, however, the Mexican group had conducted a continuing shootout with workers on the Norias (or Draw Wells) Ranch, a subdivision of the immense King Ranch that sprawled across south Texas, the very size of which frequently made it a target, in words as well as in deeds, as a symbol of exploitation and excessive power.

Although characteristic corrido vagueness and gaps in the action exist, along with names, both of place and men long since forgotten, the ballad is reasonably intact. Nor are the bandits molded into larger-than-life heroes, they remain bandits, much as the legendary Tom Dooley is more pitied than celebrated in the American ballad surrounding his life ("Hang down your head, Tom Dooley, / Hang down your head and cry, / Hang down your head, Tom Dooley, / Poor boy, you're bound to die"). Forced to evacuate the premises of the Norias on learning that Rangers were en route, the Mexican adventurers netted nothing from all their troubles, beyond perhaps a degree of immortality in the ensuing ballad. In typical coplero style, the story is told in the *Corrido de los bandidos de Las Norias,* or *Ballad of the Draw Wells Ranch Bandits.*

Corrido de los bandidos de Las Norias

Domingo, ocho de agosto,
Qué presente tengo yo,
Que en el Rancho de Las Norias
Un combate se efectuó.

El tren que viene de Brownsville
Viene dando de pitadas,

Y en ese llegaron los rinches
A buscar a los bandidos.

Por las tres de la tarde
Estaban todas bien montados,
Les decía Tomás Moseley:
—Estamos muy bien preparados.—

Bandidos de Tamaulipas,
Que se mantienen con leña,
¡Qué susto les han dado
Los rinches de la Kiñena!

Dicen que Aneste Pasaño
Es un hombre muy valiente,
Pero no ha llegado a Las Norias
A calarse con la gente.

Andará por San Benito,
Harlingen o Raymondville,
Pero a Las Norias no ha llegado
Porque el teme morir.

Domingo, ocho de agosto,
¡Que fecha tan señalado!
Llegaron a Las Tenerías
Con el fin de remudar.

Salieron de Las Tenerías
Muy alegres toditos,
¡Qué susto dieron a Osavio
Al quitarle la silla!

Pasaron por Las Canteras
Bien armados toditos,
Dicen que iban a dormir
Al punto de Los Cerritos.

Dicen que allá por el río,
En uno ratito fueron rodeados,
Les agararon a balazos,
No fueron muchos los escapados.

Vuela, vuela, palomita,
Andale para el cuartel,
Andale y diga al señor Cesar
Que volearon al "hotel."

El que compuso estos versos
No sabía lo que decía,
Estos verso son compuestos
Por los rinches y bandidos.

Ballad of the Draw Wells Ranch Bandits

Sunday, the eighth of August,
How well I remember the day!
Fighting broke out at the Draw Wells Ranch,
A battle took place in this way.

Now the train that runs from Brownsville,
Steams along with its whistle wailing,
And on it arrived the Rangers,
For the bandits they were trailing.

By three o'clock that evening,
Well mounted were all the lawmen,

Said the Ranger Thomas Moseley:
"Now then we're ready to face 'em."

You Tamaulipas robbers,
Firewood sellers the lot,
From the Rangers off the King Ranch,
Ah, what a scare you got!

'Tis said that Aneste Pasaño
Is a bold man of courage quite great,
But he hasn't come to the Draw Wells Ranch
To show everybody that trait.

He might strut around San Benito,
Or in Harlingen or Raymondville,
But he hasn't shown up at the Draw Wells
Because he fears death in their steel.

Sunday, the eighth of August,
What a most significant day!
The bandits arrived at The Tanneries,
For some horses to steal away.

Then they pulled out of The Tanneries
Happy as could be they departed,
What a scare was given Osavio
When he and his saddle got parted.

Past the waterhole at The Quarry
Fled the bandits, each one armed very well,
They would, they said, put up by nightfall
At the Little Hills stop without fail.

They say that down there by the river
They were surrounded and soon met their due,
The Rangers moved in on them shooting,
And those who escaped were but few.

Fly away, little dove, fly away now,
To the King Ranch and go state the case,
Get along now and tell the big boss there
How they all shot it up on his place.

He who compiled these verses
Knew not what he's telling strangers;
These verses are compounded
By the bandits and the Rangers.

The border itself becomes, in essence, an arbiter of moral codes and beliefs. It acts as the dispassionate evaluator of which action is that of the patriotic revolutionary; that of the brigand and thief. And in later corridos a fine line is drawn between what might be considered rational commercial endeavor on the one hand and smuggling and contraband activities on the other. The magic curtain thus affords a key to distinction between governmental autocracy and a democratic pursuit of business as usual under whatever conditions might prevail. But even honest toil, when governed by the economics of the border, itself becomes a walk of life readily subject to exploitation: Where bureaucracy runs rampant, gainful employment becomes an enterprise not only on the fringes of illegal activity but a criminal action itself.

Such aspects of life are the subject matter of later corridos of the border as the boundary becomes a settled institution and entrenches itself as an unremitting fact of life. The magic curtain of escape is the principal fact that shapes the daily life of the border populace, both permanent residents as well as transients, and the economic and political aspects of it are far-reaching. It is that which becomes the issue for the later ballads, just as it becomes the obligation of the ballad maker to recite those things that have come to pass.

The corridos faithfully unfold those epochs, even as they also immortalize the protagonists. Thus they have managed to preserve a part of the cultural transformation. Ongoing change in such a hybrid condition becomes a settled fact and fixture of life itself.

Cattle-drive tales of vaqueros in northern Anglo lands have long since been replaced by chronicles of braceros and the incidents that befall such itinerant field hands in their mechanized cavalcades to and from agricultural outposts in an alien and unfamiliar land. It thus becomes a recurrent theme—that of contract workers and their erstwhile adventures in foreign climes. It is, for many of them an adventure repeated many times over, as patent a fact of life as the economic strictures themselves that coerce men into trying over and over for seasonal labor in lonely places far from home.

It is almost militaristic in language if not in thought: the recruitment of the work gang, the younger recruits, the older hands, the signing over for another stint, reenlisting, bound over for another tour.

Typically, border corridos have epitomized the protagonists of the deeper conflict and strife of such cultural inequities that have so flavored the border country. Those have their roots in such ballads as have flavored pronouncers and insurrectionists of the likes of Catarino Garza or even Juan Cortina by some. But the latter corridos are devoid of such political dissension and ostensible revolutionary calls for change. Their aims are individual rather than social, their struggles more for personal equality and justice than for broader and more sweeping cultural reform.

The dragons that the ideal border corrido hero must slay are actually those that reach beyond class sentiment and its predilection for caste. He is in fact saddled with the responsibility of overcoming cultural prejudice as well as attitudes of devout nationalism. Indeed, those cannot be thoroughly satisfied, either north or south of the boundary, by attempts to classify hybrid sympathies and loyalties, as well as proper status in a hybrid social order. It is an altogether insecure position that such a hybrid hero occupies. But as heir apparent of revolutionary pronouncers it falls to him to continue the contest, however wholly through the defense of personal liberty and freedom.

The classic prototype has been epitomized in the *Corrido de Gregorio Cortez.* As is the case with most ballads, there are numerous variations, ranging from those that seek to unfold the entire history of the protagonist to those that do little more than sketch the high point of his career, wherein the name itself becomes the reference point, not unlike the imagery called to mind with the mention of heroic names from Robin Hood to Jesse James.

Again, too, it is not so much the story in itself that is important but rather the underlying theme that is connoted, the personal struggle against virtually insurmountable odds that the ballad itself robustly symbolizes. Tampering with it in abbreviated or condensed form makes little difference.

In short, Cortez's brief career in evading the law follows the familiar pattern of avenged injustice—that of the individual, who, by force of circumstance, has been goaded into a temporary course of outlawry as a means of saving himself from an altogether unjust situation. At the Cortez ranch, following the arrival of law officers to take young Cortez into custody on flimsy evidence of his trafficking in stolen cattle, Cortez and his brother decline to give themselves up. A gunfight ensues. Cortez's brother is killed, and Cortez believes himself to be responsible for the death of one (some versions make it more than one) of the officers. As a result, Cortez takes the only course open to him, which is flight. The career of outlaw is settled upon him at once, even though it be, as in all such classic cases of the outlaw hero, tinged with mitigating circumstances.

Thus Cortez emulates the legions of those who had fled across the border after suffering some infraction with authority and the long hand of the law. Escape across the magic curtain of the border, whether to one side or the other, however, remains one of the few fairly even-handed benefits of the great boundary and the promise of a new and different life. And even though Cortez later gives himself up, it is not until after he has fled, made the magical crossing. He has accomplished what will become celebrated in corridos as a legendary ride, coupled with almost superhuman efforts in avoiding numerous posses combing the countryside in search of him.

Ultimately, of course, and to his credit, Cortez himself recognizes the error of his ways, turns himself in to the proper authorities, serves a short sentence for his wrongdoing and settles down into what presumably would be a long life of law-abiding anonymity. In that, of course, as in all stories with the principal characters living happily ever after, there is no romance. It is in the epochal event of his young life—that of an outlaw with a reward on his head dashing off to the lonely border town of Piedras Negras, opposite Eagle Pass, in the thinly settled Rio Grande country between Del Rio and the two Laredos and the overwhelming vastness of Coahuila—that legendary romance lies. And it is the singular misadventure of his early life that forms the ballad. One of the shorter versions portrays the affair:

Corrido de Gregorio Cortez

Iba Gregorio Cortez
con su pistola en la mano:
—No siento haberlos matado,
lo que siento es a mi hermano.—

Tomó rumbo a Piedras Negras
sin ninguna timidéz:
—Síganme rinches cobardes,
yo soy Gregorio Cortez.—

Iban los americanos
que parecía que volaban
también se iban a ganar
diez mil pesos que les daban.

Decían los americanos:
—¿Si lo alcanzamos qué haremos?
Si le hablamos por la buena
muy poquitos quedaremos.—

Decía Gregorio Cortez
con su alma muy encendida:
—Pues yo no entrego mis armas
hasta estar en bartolina.—

Otro día por la mañana
él solo se presentó:
—Por la buena si me llevan,
lo que es de otro modo no.—

The Ballad of Gregorio Cortez

Gregorio Cortez went off at a gallop,
With his pistol in his hand:
"I don't regret having killed them,
It's my brother's death I can't stand."

He set off for a town on the border,
And there is no fear as he says,

"Follow me, cowardly Rangers,
For I am Gregorio Cortez."

Away went the American police force,
So fast that they seemed to fly,
For they had in mind the reward money,
The ten thousand they'd get by and by.

To themselves the Americans were saying:
"If we catch up with him, what'll we do?
If we talk to him quietly and gently,
Of we many there'll remain but a few."

Gregorio Cortez contested,
With all the fire in his soul:
"I'll never hand over my pistols
Till a jail cell itself is my goal."

But the next day, later that evening,
He gave up of his own accord,
Saying, "It's only because I am willing,
Not because you have earned the reward."

As a wrongdoer albeit with at least a modicum of justification for his actions, Cortez is not an altogether inestimable figure. He has combined a course of bravado with uprightness, nor has he carried it to the point of his behavior coming off as foolish.

Cortez, perhaps excessively conscious of his rights as an individual, is certainly more than willing to fight for them; yet he is also of a sufficiently practical turn of mind to avoid sacrificing himself when the odds are too much against him. Even in unconditional surrender the daring outlaw who set off "with his pistol in his hand" can justify his surrender as an act wholly of his own making. It is self-will over coercion backed up with relentless force.

Even subjugated, Cortez has held on to his dignity, his sense of self-worth. He has made his peace with some degree of honor, and the accomplishment of that remains a part of his own self-discipline, his personal enterprise—wrong though it was—in taking matters into his own hands.

Like the situation depicted in the *Pronunciados,* or *Insurrectionists,* idealistic causes were subject to degeneration, even to a sort of internecine feuding conducted ever and always across the magic curtain of the border. But, of course, to that they owed their origins.

Indeed, with the establishment of the border itself, three prominent phases come into play during the course of its early history and the effect it had on the general populace long resident there. First, and perhaps foremost, is the psychological quest for an ideal border type of hero, followed by a spate of pronouncements or revolutionary overtures with an eye to establishing independent border republics, and finally the backlash of patent banditry in the wake of the founding of vast estates—cattle ranches and immense land holdings—giving rise to a growing population of landless men and women stripped of the means to support themselves save through theft, which in the eyes of many simply meant repossessing that which they perceived to have been theirs originally. If a banner of idealism or revolutionary politics could be raised to go along with the undertaking, so much the better. After all, the border itself was international politics, and politics, whether in Washington or Mexico City, was so far removed as to seem almost nonexistent on the vast stage over which the magic curtain of escapist change and transformation could rise and fall.

Thus the trio of corridos here, *The Ballad of Gregorio Cortez, Ballad of the Insurrectionists* and *Ballad of the Draw Wells Ranch Bandits,* serve to demonstrate the three chief phases of early border history, the raising of the magic curtain itself. Only at a later stage would the corridos become more socially conscious in their treatment of broader problems ranging from agricultural exploitation and smuggling to illegal immigration and the "sad situation" of total unemployment as experienced during the Great Depression of the 1930s.

6

Mecca for the Landless: Life in the Fields

Although the spread of cotton farming, the American South's celebrated one-crop system, ultimately would reach to the Pacific coast, the economic and social conditions brought into play by intensive cotton production was felt early on in Texas, particularly the coastal plain of the Gulf region. For the underemployed what the introduction of so competitive and labor intensive a crop meant was the likelihood of more work. And the ranks of the underemployed were heavily staffed with Mexican immigrants as well as native-born Mexican Americans.

Cotton culture, and what it meant to be a member of either of those minority groups in competing for field work is inimitably depicted in the ballad that sings of Robstown (or Robestown, as the corrido has it), a small town near Corpus Christi on the Texas Gulf Coast. Robstown, in the hands of the *coplero,* can scarcely be praised enough, indeed, it sounds like an advertisement, a sort of recruiter's song. It is a place of storied wealth and the veritable mecca of cotton pickers inasmuch as Robstown is devoted to a single-minded purpose of making a new crop quickly, hiring everyone who wants to work, and thus benefiting all concerned.

While numerous attitudes are reflected in the ballad, the scheme of things is accepted unquestioningly and on good faith. There is no criticism of the system, and the cotton planter is lauded as the father of it all, the party who is solely responsible for creating all the jobs.

That the pay is such that entire families must join in the undertaking also is readily accepted. It is, in fact, rather to the credit of these workers of the land and its crops that so unassuming an optimism and straightforward notion of fair play on their part can prevail. Their labor can be turned almost into a competitive game for the captains of agriculture who, to the lowly cotton pickers, are wealthy beyond belief, millionaires even, according to the balladeer. The ballad, however, is not at all concerned with any sort of disparities nor inequities. No question of fairness nor wages is ever raised; rather, the verses are a panegyric to the fact that there is work, indeed, any sort of work at all, to be had.

Despite the long hours, the backbreaking labor, the low pay, the familial exploitation, there is no rancor in the corrido. The cotton pickers, in fact, are elated that there is a ready market for their labor. They are, after all, seen as a different entity, a tightly knit group quite outside the Anglo-American scheme of things, so much so that even the verses to their work song are considered to be exclusive. Knowing the words, in effect, sets one apart as having gone through a sort of initiation, a rite of passage because, as the narrator claims, they are virtually impossible to learn unless one shares in the workaday life in the fields.

A near childlike naiveté and open-mindedness prevail, enhancing the very artlessness of the agricultural work that is a way of life for the extended family. The twenty-one stanzas of *Corrido de Robestown, The Robstown Ballad,* vibrantly describe the situation.

Corrido de Robestown

Señores, voy a cantarles
este bonito corrido
del pueblo de Robestown,
pues es el pueblo más lucido.

Todos los americanos
que viven en Robestown,
toditos son millonarios,
hombres que saben gastar.

No se les puede quitar
que gastan mucho dinero
para sembrar algodón
en beneficio de los pueblos.

Por eso los mexicanos
y toditas las naciones
se vienen a Robestown
a pizcar los algodones.

En el pueblo de Robestown
se gana mucho dinero
pizcando los algodones
que siembran en ese pueblo.

Para ganarse dinero
al pueblo de Robestown
vienen muchachas bonitas
como ustedes las verán.

El que conoce ese pueblo
nunca lo puede negar
se gana mucho dinero
porque hay donde trabajar.

De todo el estado de Texas
es el pueblo más lucido
porque se gana dinero
no más como yo lo tiro.

Toda la gente, señores,
se vienen a Robestown
toditos con la intención
hay de venir a pizcar.

Hombres, muchachos y niños
ya se vienen arrimando
buscando donde pizcar
para irse ya asegurando.

Del norte se vienen muchos
de San Antonio también
a pizcar el algodón
para volverse otra vez.

Estos versos son bonitos
son del pueblo de Robestown
pues el que quiera aprenderlos
pues tiene que ir a pizcar.

Apúrese, compañero,
aprende estos versitos
pízquele pronto algodón
acabe con los surquitos.

Fúgase, compañerito,
ya nos vienen alcanzando
las muchachas morenitas
que vienen atrás pizcando.

Ya me duelen las manos
de tanto estirar capullo;
si nos alcanzan, amigo,
acabo yo no me apuro.

También los otros muchachos
que vienen atrás pizcando
vienen muy apuraditos
ya nos vienen alcanzando.

Y mi tía Josefita
que viene también pizcando
ya toditos la largaron
también agarró su paso.

También mi tío Juanito
y que es muy bien pizcador
las muchachas lo largaron
con cien libras de algodón.

En las pizcas de algodón
nadie lo puede negar
que toditos a lo menos quiere
sus cien libras pizcar.

Va a terminar el corrido
del pueblo de Robestown
que mis amigos escuchen
lo que les voy a cantar.

El corrido termino
por ciertas pruebas cabales;
este corrido fué compuesto
por don Eusebio González.

The Robstown Ballad

Gentlemen, I'm going to sing you
This beautiful little ditty
About the town of Robstown,
The most splendid of any city.

All of the North Americans
Who make Robstown their home
Are men celebrated as wealthy,
Who know how to enjoy what they own.

One cannot discount the fact that
Loads of money they spend
On the business of planting cotton,
Which benefits all in the end.

That is why all of the Mexicans
And every last nation on earth
Find themselves coming to Robstown
To pick cotton for all that they're worth.

Here in the city of Robstown
A great deal of money is made
Picking these rows of cotton
That are sown as this town's stock in trade.

To earn for themselves some money
From Robstown's bountiful pelf

Come the most beautiful maidens,
As you will see for yourself.

Whoever knows the city
Could never let it be said
That you cannot earn lots of money
Since there's plenty of work to be had.

In all of the whole state of Texas
It's the best town in every which way,
For there one can make as much money
As can I myself throw away.

Now, sirs, all of the people
To Robstown are making their way,
Every last one with the notion
Of picking some cotton each day.

Men, youngsters and children
Already in crowds are all mixed,
Selecting their spots for picking
In order to leave here well-fixed.

From up north come a great many,
From San Antonio, too,
To go out each day picking cotton,
And each day to come back anew.

Beautiful are these verses
The city of Robstown yields,
But whoever wants to learn them
Must go out to the cotton fields.

Get a move on there, companion,
Learn how each little verse goes,
Pick yourself quickly some cotton,
Get rid of those little old rows.

Hustle up there, little companion,
Those dark-haired girls to the rear,
Who are picking along behind us,
Are catching up and drawing quite near.

Already my hands are hurting
From the bolls for which I still scurry;
Friend, they're going to overtake us,
But I'm through with trying to hurry.

Even those other young fellows,
Who are picking back there to the rear,
Are moving along much faster
And will soon be abreast of us here.

Even my little Aunt Josie,
Who's going along picking, too,
Has already been passed by the others
And quickened her pace anew.

Also, my Uncle Johnny,
Who's a very good picker, indeed,
Has been outpaced by the women
With a hundred pounds of cotton and seed.

In this business of picking cotton,
There is no one who can deny
That whoever goes out picking
For at least one hundred pounds will try.

Now this ballad of Robstown
Is about to wind up right soon,
May you, my friends, now listen
To what I sing in the rest of the tune.

Herewith I finish the ballad,
With perfect rules, and no follies;
This ballad was composed by
Mr. Eusebio González.

Unqualified enthusiasm is reflected in the Robstown quatrains attributed to Eusebio González, as is claimed in the final stanza. It is a happy ballad, and Robstown itself is a happy place, which, of course, may well overstate the case and simplify matters, but the corridos of the border are accepting of life as it is, not to pick away at faults, inequities and injustices.

The *Corrido de Robestown* in particular endorses the status quo. Neither families nor ethnic groups are seen as victims of any sort of exploitive system, despite the balladeer's pointing out that all the Americans who live in Robstown are inordinately wealthy—every single one a millionaire (*"toditos son millonarios"*). Certainly the competitive spirit is accepted, even endorsed; the hard hand labor pits the old against the young, the sexes themselves rivaled against one another, as social critics might read into the verses.

But Robstown merely reflects the way things are. A cotton picker works along with—at times against—other family members, whether it be one's Aunt Josie or Uncle Johnny. Indeed, it all becomes but a part of the competitive spirit of the enterprise in which the landowners thrive, though certainly not the landless workers, inasmuch as entire families must labor in the cotton fields.

The Robstown Ballad then is altogether celebratory; the work situation itself is depicted as almost a sportive event, a contest of sorts, even a festive affair, with people—pretty girls included—coming from all over to join in the work. It has, in short, almost the elements of a state fair, and the endorsement of it all by the *coplero* is unqualified. It is a bit of living history, a folk rendering of outsiders not yet at home in the urban environment and not altogether familiar with the society and economic order in which they now find themselves. If they have passed to the other side of the magic curtain, they nonetheless have brought along older cultural trappings that are not part and parcel of a more cosmopolitan world.

Since the early 1900s the border had become an inescapable element in the lives of Mexican workers moving across it in their search for employment. While numbers of them ultimately migrated well beyond the pale of the curtain of escape, some eventually to be absorbed into the industrial populace of America and more diversified fields of industry, the majority of workers moving out through the Mexican north were agricultural laborers, and it was in that field that they usually found jobs.

Making their way into itinerant gangs of field hands, they would sign on for the duration of one harvest after another. Rates of pay even for such itinerants of Anglo origin and native born were to remain infinitesimally low, and for non-English-speaking hands (or "shoulders" as the Spanish equivalent, braceros, has it) wages were so much lower that the latter not infrequently could go in the hole, actually reaching a point of diminishing returns for their labor. At times victimized by the unscrupulous, who preyed upon their inadequacies in English, as well as by contracts and monetary exchanges, many could also be further browbeaten by threats to their mojado or wetback status since large numbers would have entered the United States illegally and remain ever fearful of deportation.

Although eventually contracts between the two nations were worked out for the admission of Mexican field hands, the quota for braceros was steadily reduced over the years. Ultimately, with intensified efforts and concerted lobbying on the part of both American labor as well as agricultural interests, the pact was abandoned in the 1960s. The virtual barring of braceros, in effect, would serve to contribute to rather than reduce the exploitation of agricultural workers.

Crop work and harvest labor, always a poorly paying proposition from the outset, would become increasingly subject to graft and chicanery, political favoritism and violence. But for poor Native Americans, and Mexican Americans in particular, poor being virtually synonymous with that ethnic classification at the time, agricultural labor remained almost the only form of labor to which they could turn. Frequently unlettered, almost habitually unskilled, year in and year out, the impoverished and disheveled caravans of nomadic harvest workers were to become increasingly a part of the American farm scene.

Yet even in that poverty-stricken past it was not fitting that such workers should be left to their own devices in selling their services. On the part of the majority of the braceros who of course came poorly equipped to defend themselves in a theoretically free labor market of a foreign land, the situation was readily perceived by those with an eye to profiting from others' hardships.

The time was ripe for further exploitation on the part of the already exploited, and the *enganchador,* the labor contractor or "hooker," was soon on the scene. Usually, if not always, a hybrid, the *enganchador* bridged the two societies, at least to the point of playing one against the other for material gain, profiting from both his bilingual expertise as well as from a general knowledge of the ins and outs of the two cultures that the magic curtain of the border comprised.

Such labor brokers, or cultural exploiters in a large sense, stood in rather much the same position as did old-time dealers in shanghaied seamen, press-ganged workers, even some modern-day recruiters for the military. In like fashion it behooved the *enganchador* to make use also of unbreakable contracts, provided they were called for at all, since in so controlled an environment escape was as foolhardy perhaps as it was unfeasible

Although later the role of *enganchador* itself would change, the word coyote eventually coming to symbolize a far more unscrupulous type of entrepreneur frequently guiding unwary would-be migrants to nonexistent jobs and even to clandestine rendezvous with death itself in sealed boxcars or the suffocating confines of enclosed trucks, for decades the *enganchador* flourished. And, as a number of border corridos testify, a sort of melancholy romanticism enshrouded the whole scheme of things.

Much of the nomenclature itself, the jargon that arises within the scope of illegitimate or quasi-illegal fields of endeavor, is militarized if not romanticized in the fashion of securing personnel for rather rough-hewn if not tough, even exotic, sorts of ventures. Nor did the field hands find themselves in any better bargaining positions than indentured types of work forces of the past. Hooked, recruited, enlisted, signed up, coerced or simply bamboozled, members of those same sorts of groups, in but seconds had signed away much of their individual rights if not indeed their very manhood.

In the recruiting of field hands, too, seldom has it been the neophyte who significantly counts; rather it has been the old hand, the veteran old-timer who returns again and again. Thus it is the ones who "re-up" and "sign over" even in the face of not too savory past experiences that become the martyrs, the reenlistees or reenganchados of the harvest gangs of seasonal workers.

It is that corps of individuals celebrated in the border corridos dedicated to celebrating the adventures of the "rehooked ones." The plaintive farewell that is the theme of *La despedida de los reenganchados* ballad, or *The Reenlistees' Farewell,* captures a leavetaking common to most all as a part of the heritage of such international migrant crop workers.

La despedida de los reenganchados

Adiós, muchachos, me voy de mi tierra,
salgo en el enganche manaña en el tren
pero llevo al frente mi fe y mi bandera
y adonde yo vaya irá ella también.

Voy a ver a los gringos para ver que quieren
con los mexicanos que vienen a traer;
al fin que los hombres dondequiera mueren
y voy a su tierra, pues que me han de decir.

Dicen que me quieren para que trabaje,
cuatro pesos dólar me van a pagar;
si es para otra cosa no crean que me raje
que también el rifle lo se manejar.

Tres meses de plazo llevo en mi contrato,
si no me conviene luego volveré;
y si son legales y me dan buen trato,
algo de más tiempo les ayudaré.

The Reenlistees' Farewell

So long, boys, I'm off from my homeland,
Leaving tomorrow on the workers' train;
But with me I'll carry my faith and my banner,
And wherever I travel, they'll go with me in twain.

To the gringos I'm going, to see what they want from
All of these Mexicans being shipped in this crew;
In the end, let the rest die wherever they want to,
Me, I'm off to their country for what they'll have me to do.

They say that they want me in order to work, and that
Four dollars American they're going to pay;
If it's for some other something, don't think I'm just bragging
When I say with a rifle I also know how to play.

Three months' time is what my contract now calls for,
If it don't suit me I'll return later on;
And if it's all legal and fair and square treatment,
I'll help them out longer before I am gone.

While the *despedida,* or farewell, sets the stage for impending departure, it is the international boundary itself, the magic curtain of certain change, which truly separates the workers, divides the men from the boys, as one might say. After all, these are veterans, reenganchados, who have done it all before; despite a certain air of insouciance, underneath there lies a bit of uneasiness, too, which is coupled with the notion that if it all does not work out, then one can get out of it.

In short, the ballad is rather self-reassuring. It is as if the balladeer must whistle up his courage in order to try to settle his own insecurities and doubts: Not only can he take care of the job he has signed up to do, he knows how to take care of himself should it turn out he has been given a bum steer as to what the work entails. Thus anxieties are soothed by what seems actually a false sense of bravado, for there are simply too many variables on the other side of the magic curtain. Even if one has worked there before, it remains an unfamiliar and, in truth, a poorly comprehended environment.

Moreover, beyond the great barrier of the border, it remains a situation in which it is every man for himself. Once there, on the other side, it is understood that the work gang will be divided and subdivided again and again, portioned out to pursue their common destiny in strange surroundings with a series of ever-changing companions along the way.

Thus the following pair of border ballads, *Los reenganchados a Kansas,* or *The Reenlistees Kansas-bound,* and the *Corrido de Pensilvania,* or *Ballad of Pennsylvania,* make common cause in recounting the quintessential fates of migrant farm workers along a shared route to employment. *Los reenganchados a Kansas* is one of the older typical ballads of work gang travel epics relating what befalls a contingent of braceros bound for the American Midwest.

Los reenganchados a Kansas

Un día, tres de septiembre,
Ay, ¡qué día tan señalado!
Que salimos de Laredo
Para Kansas reenganchados.

Cuando salimos de Laredo
Me encomendé al Santo Fuerte,
Porque iba de contrabando
Por ese lado del puente.

Uno de mis compañeros
Gritaba muy afanado:
—Ya nos vamos reenganchados
A trabajar al contado—.

Corre, corre, maquinita,
Por esa línea del Quiti,
Anda a llevar este enganche
al estado de Kansas City.

Salimos de San Antonio
Con dirección a Laguna,
Le pregunté al reeganchista
Que si íbamos para Oklahoma.

Respondió el reenganchista:
—Calle, amigo, no suspire,
Pasaremos de Oklahoma
Derechito a Kansas City.—

Ese tren a Kansas City
Es un tren muy volador,
Corre cien millas por hora
Y no le dan todo el vapor.

Yo les digo a mis amigos:
—El que no lo quiera creer,
Que monte en el Santa Fe,
A verá donde esté al amanecer.—

Al llegar a Kansas City
Nos queríamos regresar,
Porque nos dieron el ancho
Con las veras de alinear.

Decían los americanos
Con muchísimo valor:
—Júntense a los mexicanos
Para meterlos en la unión.—

Nosotros les respondimos:
—Lo que es la unión no entramos,
Esta no es nuestra bandera,
Porque somos mexicanos.

Si no siguen molestando
Nos vamos a regresar
Para el estado de Tejas
Donde hay en que trabajar.—

Agarramos un volante,
Trabajamos noche y día,
No más daban de comer
Solo purita sandía.

Vuela, vuela, palomita,
Párate en ese manzano,
Estos versos son compuestos
A todos los mexicanos.

Ya con esta me despido
Por la flor del granado,
Aquí se acaba cantando
Los versos de los reenganchados.

The Reenlistees Kansas-bound

One day, the third of September,
Ah, what a notable day!
That day we departed Laredo
Recruited for work up Kansas way.

When we pulled out of Laredo
I put myself in the Good Lord's hands,
For then I was traveling illegally
In the North Americans' lands.

Shouted one of my companions,
With plenty of verve and panache:
"Here we go signed up again, boys,
All ready to work for some cash."

Get along, get along, little engine,
Along that line they call the Kitty,

And carry this gang of yardbirds
To the state of Kansas City.

We pulled out of San Antonio
Bound for a place called Laguna,
I asked one of the old-timers
If we were going through Oklahoma.

The old reenlistee responded,
"Hush, friend, don't give in to self-pity;
We will pass right through Oklahoma,
Straight ahead on to Kansas City."

That train to Kansas City
Is a regular flying machine,
It can do a hundred miles an hour
Without giving it all the steam.

I tell friends who don't believe it
To climb aboard the Santa Fe,
If they want to see just where they'll be
When the dawn comes up next day.

On arriving in Kansas City
We wanted right off to return,
For at once we then were confronted
With some truths we never could spurn.

"Round up all of those Mexicans,"
From the Americans the cry went out,
"So we can sign them up in the union,"
They boldly the scheme sang out.

"To join this thing called a union,
We can't enter into forsworn,
Since it isn't our cause," we answered,
"Because we are Mexican born.

"If us you continue to bother,
We are going to head right on back,
Straight away for the state of Texas,
Where there's work, and of it no lack."

In a gang a flunky arranged us,
Night and day we worked in the fields,
And nothing but watermelon
Was all we got for our meals.

Fly away, fly away, little white dove,
Settle down on that apple tree twig;
These verses here were created
For all the Mexicans who went on that gig.

With that I will bid farewell now,
In the wake of these choice stanzas,
Here winds up the ballad
Of the reenlistees signed over for Kansas.

Apart from the brouhaha over the union episode, the problems related in *Los reenganchados a Kansas* are those inherent for all agricultural laborers crossing the border. Not only is there the strangeness and alien immensity of America itself to be faced, but there is also the unfamiliarity with the geographical setting, the peculiarity of names and places, towns and regions. It tumbles out in the anxiety and frustration over never knowing quite what to expect, let alone of properly grasping where one is, has been, or is going.

Inevitably, too, there is always and ever petty exploitation, but that, of course, is commonly the fate of all who step outside the more familiar platforms of ritualized authority. Chicanery at the paymaster's table, poor fare, short rations, improper accommodations, overwork—frequently any, and more often all, of those seem as inescapable as confrontations arising over economic, racial or nationalistic prejudices or combinations of all three.

Moreover, the braceros feel themselves victimized by lesser, though no less intimidating, groups of trade union organizers whose aims, motives and methods they fail to understand. In those hard-pressed times of frequent and widespread underemployment, such concepts are alien to their habits of thought as well as their way of life. It is simply too much of a foreign notion, the union thing *("lo que es la unión")*, and the Mexicans are there to work, not argue over abstractions concerning their labor. Furthermore, they are caught off balance to begin with after having undergone the difficulty of bureaucratic procedures in getting the proper papers for temporary residence, work and travel in a foreign land, difficulty often overcome only by illegal measures that serve to intensify their underlying apprehensiveness.

The advantages of unionization in agricultural labor notwithstanding, such efforts could not be supported, much less endorsed, by bracero groups, even if they were in the country legally. And in the case of Spanish-speaking Americans of Mexican descent who were migrant farm workers, the quest for unions was necessarily poorly backed and long lacking in concerted action. Although many if not most had been nurtured in the very cradle of agricultural hardship to the point that they were masters in land husbandry, little recognition was accorded for such nurturing skills.

Indeed, perhaps more often than not, such a heritage of working the land could prove to be altogether disadvantageous for both Mexican nationals and native-born Mexican Americans alike. Their very knowledge and skills coupled with an inbred sense of perfection in crop work and harvesting seemed to prohibit them from concerted efforts in labor bargaining and a seeming inability to give less than an honest day's work for wages that were never commensurate with such a perfectionist attitude. It was the penalty of perfectionism, a quality that has never led to very much in the way of job protection. And while it may have been a force in fostering a certain individualism it was only a handicap in bettering the lot of all as an ethnic minority.

A number of border corridos thus continued to put forward such an earthiness in both belief and feeling, in heritage itself concerning working the land. Much of it is romanticized, even sentimentalized. But it is a harsh romanticism, born of constant travail, hardship and the transient life fostered by migrant crop work and its built-in system of economic exploitation. Much of it is well demonstrated in the *Corrido de Pensilvania,* or *Ballad of Pennsylvania.*

Corrido de Pensilvania

El día veintiséis de abril,
a las seis de la mañana,
salimos en un enganche
pa' el Estado de Pensilvania.

Mi chinita me decía:
yo me voy en esa agencia,
para lavarles la ropa
y pa' darles su asistencia.

El reenganchista me dijo,
no lleves a tu familia,
para no pasar trabajos,
al Estado de Pensilvania.

Pa' que sepas que te quiero
me dejas en Fort West,
cuando ya estés trabajando
me escribes de donde estés.

Cuando ya estés por allá
me escribes, no seas ingrato,
de memorias yo te mando
de recuerdos mi retrato.

Adiós, Estado de Texas,
con toda su plantación,
ya me voy a Pensilvania,
por no pizcar algodón.

Adiós, Fort West de Jara,
pueblo de mucha importancia,
ya me voy a Pensilvania
por no andar la vagancia.

Al llegar a Piquileque
cambiamos locomotora,
de allí salimos corriendo
a ochenta millas por hora.

Cuando llegamos allá
y que del tren nos bajamos,
preguntan las italianas:
¿De dónde vienen, mexicanos?

Responden los mexicanos,
los que ya sabían inglés:
Venimos en un enganche
de la ciudad de Fort West.

Estos versos los compuse
cuando yo venía en camino,
son poesías de un mexicano
nombrado por Constantino.

Ya con esta me despido,
con mi sombrero en la mano
y mis fieles compañeros
son trescientos mexicanos.

Ballad of Pennsylvania

The twenty-sixth day of April,
In the morning at six o'clock straight,
We pulled out in a workers' convoy
Bound for Pennsylvania state.

My little woman kept saying,
I'm going along too on that deal,
To keep you all in clean clothing,
And prepare for you every meal.

One work gang veteran told me,
Don't gamble your family's fate,
Lest they meet up only with hardship
In Pennsylvania state.

So that you'll know I love you,
In Fort Worth leave me be,
When you're settled in where you're working,
From up there write back to me.

When you are off far away there,
Write me soon; don't make me wait!

From my heart I bequeath you my portrait
For your memories as a keepsake.

Farewell to you, State of Texas,
With all of your farm worker sops,
I'm off to Pennsylvania
So I won't have to pick cotton crops.

Farewell, Fort Worth, where the West starts,
City of fame and renown,
So I won't be counted a vagrant,
To Pennsylvania I'm bound.

On arriving at Philadelphia
We switched to a train with more power,
And from there on we continued
Running at eighty miles an hour.

When we got to our destination
And down from the train began to climb,
Some Italian women inquired of us
Where we came from down the line.

Some of the Mexicans answered,
Who in English a bit could converse,
We came up here in a work gang,
From the city of Fort Worth.

These verses, I composed them
While on the road to my fate,
They are the poetry of a Mexican
Named for Constantine the Great.

So with that I will take my leave now,
Holding my hat in my hand,
And my most faithful companions
Are three hundred Mexicans from the land.

Altogether noteworthy in the very title of the *Corrido de Pensilvania,* or *Ballad of Pennsylvania,* is the obvious celebration of the broadening of territory encompassed now in the adventures of migrant agricultural workers moving north across the border and escape across the magic curtain into quite unfamiliar regions. And in significantly large groups as well, a complement of three hundred, according to the ballad maker, Constantine, who takes credit for the verses.

Even with that slight accreditation, however, the corrido retains the typical impersonal quality inherent in the usually anonymous ballads, although a degree of sophistication, a rather more cosmopolitan air, is attained. Farewell is bid not only to the state of Texas but also to work in the cotton fields, notwithstanding the advertisement-like praises given such labor in the *Corrido de Robestown,* extolling the virtues of the grueling labor despite its association with a caste-like system even in the American Southwest where Spanish-speaking field hands had for the most part taken the place of African Americans in that one-crop industry.

Consequently, too, a more exotic atmosphere is revealed, even in getting out of Texas and its indefinitely vague though highly important town *("pueblo de mucha importancia")* of Fort West de Jara, which, however, is no less indefinite to the coupleteer than "Pensilvania" itself or even "Piquileque." It is quite enough that they are obviously faraway places, containing different groups of people—Italians—but with whom at least some of the more seasoned workers who speak English can converse. In the folk culture of balladry, one is not apt to be pinned down much on validity. As with olden lecturers, novelists and general gadabouts describing remote places prior to the Great Age of Travel and ubiquitous anthropologists, inaccuracies in names and settings were more easily accepted by less knowledgeable audiences.

7

The Periphery of Law and Order

Smuggling as well as peripheral activities in contraband are familiar themes to most dwellers on either side of the border. National as well as vested interests come into play, frequently working at cross purposes with each other. The flow of people, goods and services, of course, is always subject to change; indeed, retaliatory measures can be effected almost overnight, especially wherein extralegal activities of almost any sort seem to be getting out of hand. After all, it is the uneven quality of so many aspects of the two social orders that make the magic curtain of escape just that, both a means and a place for getting around certain restrictions, finding loopholes within the normal scheme of things.

While whole careers can be built out of trafficking in contraband, as was evident in the United States during the years of Prohibition, and later with the monumental increase in and recognition of a drug-using culture, laws as well as trends and fads in both morality and the marketplace can render such activities a seasonal if not a part-time employment. And while all infractions of the law are of course matters of degree, whether it be minor profiteering in modest monetary exchanges or murder for hire, in times of financial duress and joblessness, clandestine ventures can increase to the point that the whole of the border can become the stage on which some form or another of quasilegal or patently criminal activity occurs daily.

From illegal border crossings to blackmarketing inconsequential trinkets of open commerce, almost anyone can fall victim to infringing the law. What is worthy of attention are not those who succeed but those who get caught, the sort of glorified failure songs typified in America by *Birmingham Jail* or Johnny Cash's rendition of *Folsom Prison Blues*. For border corridos an equivalent is *El contrabando del Paso,* which perhaps is better rendered as *Song of the Smuggler.*

El contrabando del Paso

El día siete de agosto
estabamos desesperados
pues nos sacaron del Paso
para Kansas mancornados.

Nos sacaron de la corte
a las ocho de la noche,
nos sacaron para el Dipo
nos montaron en un coche.

Yo dirijí las miradas
por todita la estación
a ver si veía a mi madre,
e implorar su bendición.

Ni mi madre me esperaba
ni siquiera mi mujer,
adiós todos mis amigos,
cuando los volveré a ver.

Ya viene silbando el tren,
ya no tardará en llegar,
compañeros de mi vida,
vámonos a caminar.

Les dije a mis compañeros
al ir a montar al tren:
me encomiende al Santo Niño
que me conceda volver.

Santo Niño de Plateros,
te pido esta maravilla,
dame licencia, Niñito,
de volver con mi familia.

Al pararme en l'escalón
me hice el hombre mas fuerte,
les dice a mis compañeros:
me ha tocado mala suerte.

Es bonito el contrabando,
se gana mucho dinero,
pero lo que más me puede
son las penas del prisionero.

Ya comienza a andar el tren
ya repica la campana,
la pregunté a Mister Hill
que si vamos a Luisiana.

Mister Hill con su risita
me contesta: no, señor,
pasaremos de Luisiana
derechito a Liverpool.

Corre, corre, maquinista,
suéltale todo el vapor,
anda, deja estos coditos,
hasta el plan de Liverpool.

Yo les dije a mis amigos
que le entren a experimentar,
que en el primer contrabando
a ver donde van a dar.

Yo les digo a mis paisanos
que brinquen el charco seco
no se crean de los amigos
que son cabezas de puerco.

Que por cumplir la palabra,
amigos, en realidad,
cuando se halla uno en la cárcel
se olvidan de la amistad.

Yo le digo con razón
por algunos compañeros,
que en la calle son amigos
porque son convencieros.

Pero de eso no hay cuidado,
ya lo que paso voló,
algún día se han de encontrar
donde me encontraba yo.

Llegamos a San Lorenzo
como a las once del día,
visitamos los umbrales
de la Penitenciaría.

Unos vienen por un año,
otros con un año y día,
otros con dieciocho meses,
a la Penitenciaría.

Hay te mando, mamasita,
un suspiro y un abrazo,
mañana salgo en las filas
del contrabando del Paso.

Despedida no les doy
porque no la traigo aquí,
se la deje al carcelero
pa' que se acuerde de mí.

Ya con esta me despido,
compañeros, con un vaso,
aquí se acaba el corrido
del contrabando del Paso.

Song of the Smuggler

That seventh day of August
We were left without any hope,
For they plucked us up out of El Paso,
Bound for Kansas like cows on a rope.

At eight o'clock that evening,
Straight out of court they pulled us,
Hauled us down to the depot,
On a railroad coach they put us.

Around every part of the station
My glances I was directing,

To see if I might see my mother
And ask of her now her blessing.

But neither my mother awaited,
Nor even my own dear wife,
Farewell to you all, my comrades,
May we meet again in this life.

Now comes the train with its whistle,
Shortly it soon will appear;
Let's go, my travel companions,
Let's be moving right on out of here.

I said then to all of my comrades
While we were boarding the car:
I'm entrusting myself to the Savior,
May He let me return from afar.

Oh, Holy Son and Father,
This miracle of you I request,
Grant me permission, oh, Father,
To return to my family nest.

Standing up then to be weighed in,
I'm the huskiest one I soon learn,
I point out to my companions,
Bad luck has fallen my turn.

Smuggling is neat for the most part,
From it you earn plenty of kale,
But what I most hate to put up with
Is the lot of a jailbird's cell.

Now the train already is moving,
Its bell tinkling like a piano,
I ask Mr. Hill, the leader,
If we're going to Louisiana.

Snorting his sly little snigger,
Mr. Hill says that's not the rule,
That we'll be bypassing Louisiana
Going straight through to Liverpool.

Keep running, engineer, keep running,
Pour all the steam to it hard,
Move it, and let these poor devils
Off at the Liverpool yard.

I said then to my comrades
That now they'd be able to see,
On the first time out, in a smuggler's lot,
Just how everything soon would be.

What I was telling my brothers
Who had crossed to this side of the brig,
Was don't count on what friends might have told you,
Who haven't the brains of a pig.

To keep one's word at all cost now,
That may be among friends an old tune,
But as soon as you wind up in prison,
They forget about friendship real soon.

I say all of this quite correctly,
You know how it is with some guys,
How out in the street you're their buddy,
And you buy all their usual lies.

Yet despite all that, now it don't matter,
It's all in the past, I agree,
But someday it must be acknowledged
Exactly what happened to me.

We pulled in there up at Lawrence
In the morning, eleven a.m.,
We then made our way through those portals
Of the famous Federal pen.

Some come up for a year's hitch,
Some for a year and a day,
Others come to do eighteen months here,
Behind these towering walls of gray.

On you, my dear little mother,
A hug and a sigh I bestow,
For tomorrow I march in the ranks of
The smugglers from El Paso.

A farewell I cannot offer,
I brought none here to decree,
That I left in the hands of the jailer
Just so as to not forget me.

And with that now I will be leaving,
Just one drink, friends, ere I go,
Here then winds up the ballad
Of the smuggler from El Paso.

In the *Contrabando* ballad attributed to Guadalupe Benítez, there is much in keeping with the border corridos of revolutionary activity as seen in the *Corrido de los Pronunciados* or *Ballad of the Insurrectionists* or the picaresque adventures of the "hooked" workers, the *enganchados*, in Kansas and Pennsylvania. Once again the commonplace elements are called up: the troop-like mode of travel, the fascination with speed, with railroads. Again, too, particularly for the prisoners, there is the restricted movement, albeit for them as well it is through an alien landscape and there is not so much a premonition as an absolute certainty of long absence.

And once more, too, there is the uncertainty of place names, as usual made perhaps a little less intimidating by the practice of Hispanicizing them—San Lorenzo for Lawrence, Kansas, and even Liverpool for the famous Leavenworth. Also, the recurrence of general geographical ignorance, the *coplero* wondering if they would be going to Louisiana. Then, too, the "beauty" of contraband is noted, much as is the "beauty" of the verses themselves in the Robstown corrido pointed out, along with the refrain of earning plenty of money.

But it is not strange that much of the continuing flux in human fortune within the entire scope of the border has been due to the heritage of the boundary and its bewitching notion as magic curtain of escape beyond slow drift as well as sudden change. All of that is reflected in the five recurrent themes of revolt, social strife, migrant workers, contraband pursuits, and immigration. But then, political conflict and economic repercussion are endemic, a heritage of the area as a storehouse of hidden wealth.

Tales of lost gold and silver mines and buried treasure have been legion since the coming of the Spaniards and their incessant quest for riches embodied in such myths as that of a gilded El Dorado, or the fabled wealth of the Seven Cities of Cíbola. It would become a part of the heritage of much of the whole vast area of the lands encompassing the farther western sector of the border and its storied bonanzas.

And there was wealth to be had, quite apart from the eventual discovery of gold in 1848 in California to which the routes of the early Spanish explorers had led, across the formidable terrain of the western Sierra Madre and the arid wastes above the headlands of the Sea of Cortez, or Gulf of California. But it was wealth of a different sort, principally copper—and precious little gold and silver—that was to be strip mined out of areas in southern Arizona and northern Sonora.

While mining operations were to become the sole industry at such border towns as Douglas, just across the line from Agua Prieta, and Bisbee, just above the twin border towns of Naco, Arizona, and Naco, Sonora, there were American-dominated land and mining operations below the border, too. Exploitation of Mexico by foreign elements, and especially Americans, had been encouraged during the long years of Porfirio Díaz's presidency, which was to topple only with the outbreak of the Mexican Revolution in 1910. Indeed, one of the fashionable arguments at the time was that foreign capital and foreign-controlled enterprises were rapidly developing Mexico and creating widespread employment.

There was, of course, a ring of truth to the statement. In the wake of such busy activity, jobs necessarily were created, but by and large the jobs available to most native Mexicans were principally those which foreigners not only did not want but even refused to do. Moreover, the wages for such employments were grossly inferior in comparison to the salaries paid foreigners, again, mostly Americans. Nor were native workers trained for upper echelons of responsibility and career advancements.

Indeed, a colonial-like habit of mind ran rampant as foreign capital and foreign-run enterprises came to dominate the country. Professional men, particularly Americans, from geologists to civil and mining engineers, along with risk-venture capitalists and entrepreneurs of varying degree of financial resourcefulness and business ethics basked as favored technocrats in the glow of the Porfirian years. In the north of "Old Mexico" in particular, spectacular personal empires in land and cattle companies flourished while throughout most of the republic there were ongoing and highly profitable—at times enormously so—ventures in mining and petroleum.

Nor was the border itself, most alien entrepreneurs had discovered, any barrier to their activities. During the lengthy and glorified years of the Porfirian heyday in benevolent dictatorship, the so-called Porfiriato, it was in fact more of a magic curtain than ever. At least for the enterprising few. For the rest, which is to say for Mexicans in general, the curtain had been drawn pretty tightly against them. Rurales, Díaz's authoritative and widespread secret police force, would see to the status quo in maintaining a docile labor force within the boundaries of the nation. And for those who transgressed such authorities, the *ley fuga,* or law of flight, was a common practice: prisoners were urged—nay, demanded—to escape, then fatally shot while doing so. The counsel of the carrot or the stick had become in essence the law of the land. *Pan o palo*—bread or stick—had become the maxim for getting along, the *ley fuga* the ultimate consequence in failure to heed such a guideline. In effect, general serfdom prevailed for exploitation of the economy by favored alien guests.

The situation would of course change in wholesale fashion with the fall of Porfirianismo and the chaotic years of the Mexican Revolution lending impetus to thousands, ultimately hundreds of thousands of Mexican nationals crossing over the magic curtain of escape into the United States during the decades of 1910 and 1920. And, too, with eventual expropriation measures and an end to the bulk of prior foreign concessions granted, a general exodus of Americans, and their capital, so favored during those years, would follow, too. However, a few remained.

One who did was William Cornell Greene, a resourceful entrepreneur who had migrated west from his native state of New York where service of a sort with the state militia had aided him in perpetuating his claim to the title of colonel and a seemingly natural-born penchant for derring-do in the realm of high financial dealings. Eventually, setting himself up in northern Sonora,

Colonel Greene soon built a personal empire in mining, land and cattle activities centered around his soon-famous headquarters, the House of Seven Chimneys, near the town of Cananea, some fifty miles south of the border and centered almost on a parallel between the dominant border towns of Douglas and Agua Prieta and the twin towns that are both named Nogales, or ambos Nogales, as frequently referred to.

Cananea during Greene's most fruitful years was almost an American town with a patrimonial social climate. A part of that is conveyed in the *Corrido de Cananea.* The Cananea environ was a distinctive atmosphere, well reflected in the disdainful aplomb and insouciant voice of the narrator.

Corrido de Cananea

Voy a dar un pormenor
de lo que a mí me ha pasado:
que me han agarrado preso,
siendo un gallo tan jugado.

Me fuí para el Agua Prieta
a ver quien me conocía,
y a las once de la noche
me aprehendió la policía.

Me aprehendieron los gendarmes
al estilo americano:
como era hombre de delito
todos con pistolas en mano.

Me enviaron a Cananea
atravesando la sierra,
no me les puede pintar
por no conocer la tierra.

Al llegar a Cananea
allí perdí la esperanza;
porque allí fuí consignado
al Juez de Primera Instancia.

Al otro día por la mañana
nos raparon la cabeza,
porque me iba a visitar
'l' administrador de mesa.

Me sacaron un recibo
de la Casa del Congreso,
donde preguntaba el juez:
—¿Sabe usted porqué está preso?—

Yo le contesté muy serio,
poniéndome muy formal:
—No me han de formar un templo
ni un palacio de cristal.—

La cárcel de Cananea
se edificó en una mesa
y en ella fuí procesado
por causa de mi torpeza.

De tres amigos que tengo
ninguno me quiere hablar,
comenzando por El Chango,
El Leoncito y El Caiman.

Despedida no la doy
porque no la traigo aquí,
se la dejé al Santo Niño
y al Señor de Mapimí.

Ya con esta me despido
por las hojas de un granado;
aquí se acabó el corrido
de este gallo bien jugado.

Ballad of Cananea

I'm going to relate you an incident,
How in times past I was put behind bars,
How they made me a man imprisoned
For being wise in the way of life's scars.

I'd taken off for Agua Prieta
Just to see who might know me up there;
And at eleven o'clock of that very same night
The police acquainted me with their care.

The gendarmes took me in custody
In the familiar American style,
Just like I was a common criminal,
Carrying weapons, and socially vile.

They carted me off to Cananea
—All unfamiliar country to me—
So I could not have checked out if they'd let me,
Not knowing the right way to flee.

On arriving in Cananea
I lost all the hope I could budge;
For right off my duty was told me:
Appear before the Primary Court Judge.

The next day, early that morning,
They shaved my whole head because later

The Periphery of Law and Order

I'd been singled out for a visit
With the business administrator.

They shook me down then for a statement,
As the law of the land requested,
And to me then the judge put the question:
"Do you understand why you've been arrested?"

I answered in manner most thoughtful
With as much respect as I could:
"Surely not to make of my body a temple
Nor heavenly host with which to do good."

The jail there at Cananea
Was built on a small low bluff,
And it was there that I was indicted
Because of my boorish guff.

Of the only three friends that I have now,
Perhaps the less said the better,
Beginning with Monk, then Tiger,
And Sharpie the Alligator.

I can't show my discharge papers,
Those I could not bring along in my haste,
I left them to the good Lord Jesus,
And the God of that great northern waste.

So with that I will now make my exit,
Like a page from a book full of strife;
For here this winds up the ballad
Of one wise in the ways of life.

8

Subculture of Salvation

Few nations are more closely attuned to the life and times of America than is its neighbor Mexico, particularly the northern tier of states that open onto the border. It is not totally dependent, nor to the point that, as has been said, when the United States suffers a cold, Mexico sneezes, but certainly the effects are felt. Sanctions and reprisals are always part of the social and especially the political climate existing between the two countries. What boils up in one spills over into the other.

Now and then effects of the political and economic order have been brought about in ongoing exchanges of people, some day to day, some temporary, many, of course, of a personal nature. Wholesale migrations in particular had come about during the years of the Mexican Revolution, and indeed continued on into the early 1930s—the period following the overthrow of Porfirio Díaz, the tense times of World War I, including the uneasiness that prevailed along the border after the intrusion of what were alleged to be troops of Pancho Villa into United States territory at the near border town of Columbus, New Mexico, and President Woodrow Wilson's ensuing deployment of American forces into

Mexico to "catch" Villa, an unsuccessful foray that proved hard to live down. Better times would follow during the 1920s, and mass immigration of Mexicans into the United States would continue during that decade. But the coming of the Great Depression in 1929 would propel Mexico, too, into the front ranks of peoples suffering from the stagnant economic climate.

While the shock waves following the Great Crash of 1929 were soon to be felt almost everywhere in the world, among the front-line casualties of the collapse of the economic system were, of course, the United States itself and its highly sensitively attuned neighbor Mexico. The beginning of at least a decade of sorrowful years was at hand as the spectre of the Great Depression began to stalk the land.

Much, of course, has now been made of the grim depravity of it all: armies of the unemployed, bread lines in Chicago, soup kitchens in New York, former corporate moguls turned street corner sellers of penny pencils, the heart-sickening exodus of "Okies" and other destitute migrants into California, the near disappearance of money itself in a monetary-based culture. Although the desperate climate of the Depression was more obvious in the heavily populated and highly industrialized East it was no less rampant and ravaging along the border, which once had provided not only escape but salvation across the magic curtain to "the other side." Indeed, in some instances, it perhaps was worse, particularly for ethnic minorities already at the bottom rung of the economic order.

Apart from the obvious hunger and homelessness brought on by joblessness and no funds, there was as well the loss of dignity coupled with a resulting sense of guilt for "failing" in the economic marketplace itself and the frustration over failing to understand why it all had happened in the first place. While corridos are not noted for overstating a case, in 1931 one of the border ballads aptly, if understatedly, described it as a "sad situation." On the whole, the *Corrido de la triste situación*, or *Ballad of the Sad*

Situation, is highly reflective of the depth of the worldwide depression and the intensity of it along both sides of what long had been the magic curtain of escape.

Corrido de la triste situación

Señores, tengan presente,
pongan mucha atención,
Voy a cantarles los versos
de esta triste situación.

El novecientos treintiuno,
¡ay! señores, ¡qué dolor,
qué miseria se presenta,
qué nos ampare el Señor!

En Ciudad Juárez sumira,
ya es cosa de lamentar,
que anda toda la gente
que no haya en que trabajar.

Madre mía de Guadalupe,
Madre mía de los Dolores,
en este Juárez ingrato
no más se oyen los clamores.

Uno al otro se decía:
esa trampa no la supe,
unos van al Porvenir,
otros van a Guadalupe.

Pues vienen del Porvenir,
de Guadalupe también,

diciéndole a sus familias:
que no encontraron que hacer.

Andan por todas las calles
prendiditos, quien los ve,
andan colectando el cinco
para tomar un café.

Llega la gente del sur
sacando sus pasaportes,
y lamentan su fortuna
en las fronteras del Norte.

Se pasan pa'l otro lado
creyendo que son formales,
y allá tan mal que los ven
los ingratos federales.

Ay, ¡qué ingratos Patones!
ya a la gente vuelvan loca,
metiéndose por los ranchos
y llevándolos en troca.

Luego que ya los agarran
les hacen observaciones,
por caminos y condados,
esos ingratos Patones.

Los llevan a Emigración
los sentencían a la corte,
los que van de contrabando
aunque llevan pasaporte.

Pobrecitos prisioneros
que a la corte van a dar,
a tomar agua caliente
y luego avena sin sal.

Cuando cumplen su sentencia
al Puente vienen a dar,
con su corazón alegre
a volver a experimentar.

Anden, ingratos Patones,
que no tienen compasión,
ya viene Alemania y Rusia
unidos con el Japón.

En la Colonia Reforma
lamentan la situación,
por los fuertes temporales
se les perdió el algodón.

El día siete de septiembre
¡qué suerte sin compasión!
que en San Francisco Tresjacales
fué la grande anegación.

Agraristas de este valle
ya no hallan ni que pensar,
quieren entregar las tierras
y salirse a experimentar.

En San Isidro y Sauzal
están acabando su vida,
pues no hallan ni que vender
para la Cooperativa.

Porbrecitos Sauzaleños,
son dignos de compasión
ya no les vale la leña
ni las ventas de carbón.

La Forestal les exige
el permiso con razón,
luego, si no lo presentan,
decomisan el carbón.

Ellos tienen esperanzas
como la flor de alelía,
que si les echan drenaje
otras cosechas tendrían.

Ya me despedido de Juárez
de la Frontera también;
ya el Gobierno nos dió pases,
ya nos vamos en el tren.

Ya con esta me despido
encogido el corazón
aquí termina el corrido
de esta triste situación.

Ballad of the Sad Situation

Gentlemen, bear this in mind now,
Lend me your undivided attention,
I'm about to recite you some verses
Concerning this sad situation.

Subculture of Salvation

The year nineteen hundred and thirty-one then,
Ah, what poverty still without end!
What misery it lays upon all of us,
May the good Lord his blessings us send!

In this City of Juárez it's depressing,
Long since it's a thing very sad,
The way people are going around here
Without any work to be had.

Virgin Mother of Guadalupe,
Holy Mother of the Incarnate Word,
In this thankless City of Juárez
Nothing but sorrow is heard.

One man to another was saying:
I didn't fall into that trap,
The way some drink it up at The Future,
While others lap up that saintly crap.

Well, they come back from The Future,
And from saying their prayers, too,
Telling the same thing to their families:
That they still have found no work to do.

They walk the streets of the city,
Put the bite on whomever they see,
Go around begging a nickel
For the price of a cup of coffee.

People come up from south Mexico,
Putting their passports in order,
Complaining about their misfortune
Up here on the northern border.

To the other side they cross over,
Believing they're clear on credentials,
But no sooner there than they see how
Corrupt are the border officials.

Ah, those big-footed ingrates,
They're driving the people quite mad,
Sniffing around all the ranches,
Grabbing whatever illegals there are to be had.

Later on, once they have seized them,
They conduct their investigation,
All those big-footed ingrates
Watching every last road in the nation.

Off they haul them to Immigration,
Sentence them there in the courts,
The ones who crossed over illegal
Although they have their passports.

Poor little unfortunate prisoners,
Them the courts will award without fault,
A cupful of hot drinking water
And later some mush with no salt.

Then, when they finish their sentence,
To the border they'll take them straight back,
Them with their hearts now gladdened
To give crossing back over another crack.

Off with you, big-footed ingrates,
You haven't one drop of compassion,
And now here comes Japan and the Russians
Teamed up with the German nation.

In all the Reforma district
They're mourning the situation,
Since it's cost them all of their cotton
Due to seasonal variation.

In tiny, impoverished St. Francis,
What a terrible stroke of fate,
The great deluge which occurred there
That seventh of September date!

Farmers throughout this whole valley
Find their thoughts now reduced to one whim,
They just want to hand over their farmlands
And then pull out, sink or swim.

In San Isidro and Sauzal, too,
They're waiving their true right to live,
Since they haven't one thing they can sell to
The Farmers' Cooperative.

Poor little Sauzal people,
They deserve pity from whatever soul,
Now they can't even sell off their cordwood,
Much less sell off any charcoal.

To do that, the Forestry Commission
Exacts, in accord with its role,
Their permission, and if they don't give it,
It simply confiscates the charcoal.

Still, though, they have all their hopes up,
Like flowers ready to bloom,
If they could only have irrigation,
For other crops soon they'd find room.

Me, I'm parting company with Juárez,
And the border country, too,
Now the government's given us passes,
Now we're off on the next train through.

So with this I'm making my exit,
Heartsick of all this privation,
Here winds up the ballad
About this sad situation.

In the *Corrido de la triste situación,* ballad maker Leonardo Leiva has sketched some of the fundamental problems that have beset inhabitants of the border country almost from the beginnings of the Old Spanish Borderlands. Those, of course, range from racism and nationalism to financial repercussions; but always and ever they are ultimately concerned with the clandestine crossings of people and goods.

The economics of exploitation and profiteering from others' misfortunes have begun to compose the essential makeup and character of the boundary area. Here is the final impasse. To the hopeful, to visionary would-be immigrants, even to transients with no particular goal, further movement is restricted by the fait accompli of the border itself. Left only are those, as voiced in the *Ballad of the Sad Situation*, who can lament the whole state of affairs for what it is and press on, having determined not to linger, but rather to quit the border country for once and all. For those of a less decisive nature, or perhaps beset with less drive and inclination to turn back, there is left to them not even that option. Already they are mired in the Third World economy of the border country, which, in effect, tolerates, rather than accepts and absorbs, their presence.

But always it works both ways. Later, as the "sad situation" straddled the border and became embodied in the worldwide spread of economic depression, the once-magic curtain fluttering over the escape route of the border would beckon again as it became the goal not only of itinerants fleeing Mexico but also of earlier migrants then seeking to flee from poverty-stricken areas of the United States as well. Once more the border had become the symbol of hope, of freedom for those who would return to mother Mexico.

The magic curtain would part, welcoming those who had left to come back in. Once more the border must reckon with repercussions brought about by humanity's migratory bent. The Great Depression itself would be the catalyst signaling a return to one's roots; migrants would pass back through the magic mirror, the enchanted looking-glass world reflected in the great international boundary. It is a theme taken up in the *Corrido de inmigración, The Immigration Ballad.*

Corrido de inmigración

Señores, voy a cantarles
con dolor del corazón
lo que sufre nuestra raza,
causa de la inmigración.

Por cuestión del Presidente
o las grandes compañías,
desocupan mucha gente
todos los más de los días.

Por lo escasez de trabajo
o casos comprometidos,
abandonan sus hogares
pa' salir de Estados Unidos.

Desde el año viente y tres
hasta la fecha en que estamos,

eso duro la bonanza,
pero ahora si ya nos vamos.

En San Francisco y San Diego
no haya la gente que hacer,
ocurren al Comité
a que les den de comer.

Los mexicanos se van
por la falta de quehacer,
van para su patria libre,
fué la que los vió nacer.

Unos van con sus familias
como se presenta el caso,
y otros van deportados
de California hasta El Paso.

En las plantas de cemento
o en obras de construcción
se junta gente de a diario
que parece procesión.

En el Valle San Joaquín
hasta duele el corazón
de ver las pobres familias
ahora en la inmigración.

Unos van a San Francisco,
otros al Valle Imperial,
los jefes de inmigración
del gobierno federal.

Andan miles por las calles

toditos descoloridos,
no más pintando mónitas
en los Estados Unidos.

Unos ya son comunistas,
otros platican de guerra,
y están deseando el pasaje
pa' regresar a su tierra.

Vuela, vuela, palomita,
con tu sombrero en las manos
dé noticias a Ortíz Rubio
que allá van los mexicanos.

Ortíz Rubio les promete
de la Frontera pa' allá,
que al mexicano que salga
su pase se le dará.

Unos van cantan y cantan
otros pobres van dormidos,
pensando en su Propriedad
que quedó en Estados Unidos.

Unos andan asustados
les dicen a sus hermanos,
que si quieren trabajar
tienen que ser ciudadanos.

En Mexicali y Nogales,
en Piedras Negras y El Paso
se ven muchas compatriotas
que van para el terrenazo.

En el pueblo San Fernando,
esto no es cosa de risa,
allí bloquearon el pueblo,
el miércoles de ceniza.

Hicieron un gran alarme,
tengan esto muy presente,
en el Barrio del Rebote
allí juntaron la gente.

Exigían el pasaporte,
mujeres, niños llorando;
se llevaron a mi papá,
sólo Dios sabe hasta cuando.

Ya con esta me despido,
les encargo, mexicanos;
hay que volver a la patria
donde están nuestros hermanos.

Es muy triste, compañeros,
vivir en estas esferas,
donde tienen que humillarse
a las ideas extranjeras.

Hay que salir de este pais
toditos a nuestra tierra,
para no prestar lugar
a que nos echen pa' 'fuera.

El que compuso estos versos,
ése se fué en aeroplano,
lleva ganas de pisar
a su suelo mexicano.

The Immigration Ballad

Gentlemen, I'm going to tell you,
From my heart so sad and cheerless,
About that which our people are suffering
Because of this immigration business.

Whether it's a presidential matter,
Or one of big business, it's clear
That a lot of people are jobless
For the better part of the year.

Because of the scarcity of employment,
Or disputes about work and pay rates,
They are giving up even their homes now
In order to leave the United States.

Ever since nineteen twenty-three now,
Right up till this very day,
For that long a time lived prosperity,
But now from us it's getting away.

In San Diego and San Francisco
There's no work for people to do;
It falls to some government bureau
To feed them enough to get through.

Mexicans are all getting out of there,
Because of jobs there is now such a dearth,
Going back to their own free country,
To the land which has given them birth.

Some are moving out with their families,
Or alone, as the case may be,

Still others are getting deported,
From California to Texas, for free.

Workers from all the cement plants,
Gangs of laborers in construction,
Join up with those moving out daily
Like a caravan in full production.

Out in the San Joaquín Valley
You can watch till it makes your heart sore,
Now in the full wake of migration
Poor families moving out by the score.

Federal government bosses
Of the immigration officers' tally,
Some go to check up on San Francisco,
Others, the Imperial Valley.

Everyone washed-out and pallid,
Strung out on the roads for miles,
No more duped by deceptions
Of the United States and its wiles.

Some already are communists,
Others talk open warfare,
Wishing they had passage money
To get back to their own land, they declare.

Fly away, fly away, little white dove,
Holding your hat in your hands;
Tell all the federal officials
The Mexicans are going back to their lands.

The federal officials assure them
That the trip from the border is free
To any Mexican making the journey
To go back to his native country.

Singing, some go along singing,
Others daydream of their fates,
Thinking about their properties
They left behind in the United States.

Walking on, jumpy and frightened,
Some say to each one they meet,
That if they want to work in America
They must be citizens or they cannot compete.

In Mexicali, Nogales, Piedras Negras,
And El Paso and points in between,
Thousands returning to Mexico,
In all border towns they are seen.

In San Fernando, California,
And this is no laughing event,
There they blockaded the entire city,
On Ash Wednesday, the first day of Lent.

There where were gathered the people,
In a ghetto called The Rebound,
A grand alarm was effected,
Just listen, here's what was found.

Passports then were demanded,
Women crying, kids making a din;
They carted away my own father,
For God only knows until when.

With that I'll take my leave now,
And I hereby all Mexicans charge:
We have to return to our homeland
Where our own people remain at large.

It's very sad, my companions,
To live in conditions like these,
Where one has to be humiliated
By any foreign idea that you please.

We have got to get out of this country,
Each one back to his own native land,
So we don't have to grovel for living space
From which they kick us off at firsthand.

He who composed these verses
Left here traveling aboard a plane,
With hope of again setting foot on
His beloved Mexican terrain.

With simple dignity, the *Corrido de inmigración* weighs the bitter harvests so long reaped by those who have crossed—transgressed—the great rift of the Americas. It is a song of a people not so much displaced as dispossessed, driven into a rationale of nationalistic fervor in order to retain a final vestige of identification, in a time of utter destitution, the one thing not stripped from them.

Although there are many other border corridos worthy of attention as mirrors of the magic curtain, it would be beyond the scope here to do more than allude to the tremendous body of corridos in the Mexican north as well as on "the other side" of the border. The international boundary itself provides the backdrop, the framework upon which the themes are stretched—tales of immigration, of contrabandists, shanghaied workers, migrants ever in trouble with the law. The border remains a zone of inquietude and transience, a place of drift and widespread temporality and, perhaps above all, of incessant movement.

With time, of course, all of that would change, like clothing styles themselves as well as contraband fads in narcotics, in drugs, in pharmaceuticals, in illicit boundary crossings. The border, the magic curtain itself, would become a harder, a tougher place, its once element of glamour receding all the more into an all but forgotten past when life and human migration were less constrained and the world on either side of the border was indeed a smaller world, and in many ways a less harsh one as sophistication in profiteering on all aspects of the human condition mushroomed and the entire framework for coping with the loopholes of both international law and customs and bureaucracies solidified into a highly commercialized subliminal culture all its own.

But the magic curtain is no less a vital threshold to those who daily cross to and from the scores of dual towns and cities, workers and employers alike capitalizing on the unevenness of the two economies, in labor, in prices, in living conditions themselves. And as ever it is a place of visitors, of shoppers, travelers, adventurers in search of that evanescent difference that is always believed to exist, somehow, on the other side of the curtained stage of the long boundary.

Yet, changes notwithstanding and increasing sameness and standardization in habits of life and thought, the border retains its elixir of enchantment. Things really are different on either side of it and so long as the international boundary endures life and thought always will be. Where there is fusion, it is into a hybrid status, into something that has not been heretofore, and beyond the expansive backdrop of the magic curtain fusion does not exist at all, neither in the shadows nor the wings. It is as illusory in the present as in the past. But reality exists in the illusion itself; were it not so, then the magic curtain of escape would have been drawn long ago.

Part Three:

The Prose

9

Southern Rim of the Western Novel

Novels, like so much else nowadays, have come to be classified, if not graded, into any number of categories, at times so superficially that the web of intercultural themes of border-country literature have been all but lost in the rush to pigeonhole, to generalize. Yet there are a number of works that resist such efforts, a body of fiction that continues to portray the essence of the magic curtain of escape, of rebirth, of hybridization and, sometimes unintentionally, of the divisive character of the great boundary of the Americas.

Cultural rift is at the core of their being, and thus there is considerable effort on the part of the novelist to introduce both sides of the magic curtain—the Rio Grande or Río Bravo, and the long, thin international line. A disparate country, it is true, and still not really well known enough to resist making literary capital of it all; a harsh country dotted with random oases, and from sea to sea sprinkled with deserts and sandy wastes as gray-green as the color of maguey, high plateaus and barrier mountains, and always the chaparral or brush country.

And yet it is there, more than anywhere else in the Americas, that an ongoing evolvement, an intercultural flowering still takes root, blossoms, even bears fruit. The magic curtain retains its magicality, on both sides. Because, in fact, of the very nature of the whole of its topography and the relative sparsity of population, apart from the larger border cities and the heterogeneity therein, its bewitching qualities endure. Despite the intrusions of anthropologists, adventurers and exotic-minded literati, the enchantment within the realm of the magic curtain prevails. If the present is too exacting, there is always the nebulous past. Thus one of the more recent attempts to exploit its historical aspects is *Fandango* by Ron McCoy (1984), while one of the older efforts is that of the early-twentieth-century novelist Will Levington Comfort in *Somewhere South in Sonora* (1925).

Comfort's *Somewhere South in Sonora* contains all of the elements of a border novel, and more—Mexican bandits and rurales, a gold mine, cowboys, immense ranchos, mythical oil wells presided over by an expatriate American ("Mexicali" Burton) in a mythical booming oil town in Sonora, plus a hybrid hero (half-Mexican, half-American) who has fled to Mexico after a murder charge was filed on him. There is even a trio of girls sojourning in Sonora (on vacation from their finishing school in Tucson), and, of course, the youthful protagonist from the East who, in the end, will set everything right.

And, to Comfort's credit, there are honest reflections on the racial antagonism seemingly inherent in the border country. An older character explains: "We used to call 'em greasers and shoot 'em up a lot, not thinking much about it. We used to hang 'em for hoss thieves, when a sheriff wanted to make a showin'. Thought little more of 'em than a Chinee, only diff'rent. Young punchers and miners—we thought we was the people. . . ."

That is what old Bob Leadley tells young Elbert Sartwell, who has come out from the East, intent on discovering the romance and legend of the great Southwest he has gleaned from books, even though Elbert's father has told him there is no longer any such West, that Elbert is thirty years too late. But Elbert persists in his dream, gets to Tucson, even secures a job with the HCO (Heaslep and Company) Ranch, a big spread, "stretching almost to the border."

As a neophyte ranch hand Elbert suffers the usual indignities of a tenderfoot (once assigned the task of filling in gopher holes with newspapers), but gradually he is accepted and becomes friends with longtime cowboys Cal Monroid and Slim Gannon.

Although later Elbert decides to return home, he first travels to Los Angeles and by happenstance obtains a job in a leather goods store. There he chances to meet the garrulous Leadley, an old prospector who finally has struck it rich at his Dry Cache mine and now is a frequent customer at the store.

Proud of his claim, but understandably guarded about its location as well as its product, Leadley avers that one could almost call it a gold mine. Southeast of Los Angeles, his diggings are high up in the mountains, and, true to the border and its magic curtain atmosphere, Leadley adds that from the site where he hit pay dirt one can see California as well as Sonora.

Finding an attentive ear, the elderly mine owner reminisces further, explaining how his only son, Bart Leadley, ran off years ago and disappeared in Sonora. Bart, the older Leadley says, would be about the same age and build as Elbert, which is what attracted him to Elbert in the first place. The old man has a proposition: Leadley wants to find his son so that he can leave him all he owns, the mine as well as a substantial amount of money in a bank. Will Elbert go look for Bart? He will. Leadley draws up the necessary papers, willing Elbert, too, a stake in the mine as well as providing for all expenses he will incur in his search for the lost son.

Bob Leadley himself had gone down to Mexico to try to find his son but the rurales had taken a special interest in his case once they learned he was looking for a white man said to be riding with the famous outlaw Monte Vallejo. Consequently the father had been forced to give up his quest. All of that is explained to Elbert by Mort Cotton, Leadley's former prospecting partner and long-time friend. Now a well-to-do rancher, Cotton and his ranch are Elbert's first rendezvous and port of call on his impending mission.

Cotton is convinced that a man named Letchie Welton informed the rurales about Leadley and his search for Bart. Welton, Cotton tells Elbert, had been sheriff back in Bismo, Arizona, the fictional town in which Leadley had lived and mined and had the son, Bart, by a Mexican woman.

The narrator of the novel explains the social barrier that existed in the fictional border town where, in the placer mines, "Mexican laborers worked, two to one to the white men." Apart from working hours, however, there was rarely any social contact. Only when "waves of drink inundated the white miners" would they "move over to Dobe-town to drink and 'eat different,' the calls ending in a row, not infrequently in the death of a 'greaser.'"

All the while, Bart was growing up "more Mexican than white," and Bart's father later admits to himself that he had been too hard on his son all along. The stage is set for young Bart's flight through the magic curtain when the Bismo storekeeper is killed and robbed. Sheriff Welton suspects a trio of Mexicans and pursues them with a posse, including the two Leadleys. When one of the Mexicans, Palto, a close friend of Bart, is critically wounded by Welton and dying in agony, Bart administers the *golpe de gracia,* mercifully killing Palto.

Welton always believed Bart had been in on the robbery and murder of the storekeeper to begin with; thus Bart is now propelled into striking out for a new life in Mexico, never again to see his father. Drifting into a bandit life in Sonora is partially justified; Cotton himself paints a picture of the unevenness of the times there, and of the rurales in particular, and the bandit leader Vallejo, who might easily have been fashioned from the mold of Pancho Villa. In short, the people love Vallejo and well have cause to hate the highhanded governmental police force of rurales "who lord it over 'em and feel important, havin' the law on their side," Cotton explains to Elbert.

For his mission, Elbert will need a faithful steed, and he soon is gifted with a marvelous horse belonging to the older Leadley and stabled on Cotton's ranch. Cotton even teaches Elbert the finer points of horsemanship and maps out the way for him to enter Sonora. Cotton suggests that Elbert ride east from San Forenso, a fictional Arizona border town, and cross into Mexico at Nogales. Luckily, it is an area Elbert already is familiar with, thanks to his work on the Heaslep Ranch.

After a spate of adventures, Elbert does succeed in finding Bart. Each, it turns out, becomes the savior of the other in recrossing the magic curtain, getting back to the States—and to Bart's heritage, the money bequeathed him by his father and a majority share in the old man's Dry Cache mine, the older Leadley having died not long after Elbert set out on his quest.

Meanwhile, however, both young men have sustained serious wounds but recovered, with Bart being nursed back to health by a young Mexican woman at whose family hacienda they took refuge, and for whom romance has blossomed. Even Elbert has met the love of his life, Mary Gertling. She is one of a trio of young women in a touring car, the three bound for Mexico to visit with the father of one of the girls, Florabel Burton, daughter of Mexicali Burton, now fighting off "all of Sonora" to keep his oil wells.

Prior to all of this, Elbert's former co-workers at Heaslep, Cal and Slim, have joined up with Elbert on his trek into Sonora in search of Bart. Indeed, the pair help him and the girls in their touring car run through a line of disgruntled Mexicans at the mythical town of San Pasquali, Burton's headquarters for his enterprises. It is during that explosive situation that Elbert is wounded but still manages to get the automobile and the three young women safely back to Tucson.

It is only later that Elbert encounters Bart, after yet more adventures and with Elbert on the point of paying with his life for having crossed the magic curtain. The rurales lock up Elbert at the cuartel in fictional Arecibo, where he is the questionable guest of Captain Ramon Bistula. Other prisoners there, members of the Vallejo band, already have been executed. A few remain; it is to free those that Bart and other stalwarts of the bandit group arrive one night to engineer their escape, including that of Elbert, when the would-be savior of Bart learns that the erstwhile leader of the bandit cadre is Bart himself.

Plot here is almost everything. The novel reads like the script for a B-grade movie, a television film or a boys' adventure tale. It is a prototype for the magic curtain, filled with Robin Hood-like Mexican bandits, courtly but cruel rurales, fictional oil wells, American cowboys, a gold mine, romance (native American as well as intercultural), the rescue of Elbert by Bart who in turn is saved by Elbert. Bart, the hybrid Mexican-Anglo, is now returned, reborn into a new and noncriminal life. Indeed, his salvation is near perfect; now obviously a man of great wealth back in the United States, he is soon paired with the young Mexican woman from El Relicario (The Shrine, appropriately) hacienda who took care of him after he was shot up by the rurales. And Elbert, too, has again found his true love, Mary Gertling, in Tucson.

Somewhere South in Sonora is indeed so borderish that it could not exist without the trappings of the magic curtain as the stage for the whole tale. While some of the place names are real, many are fictional: Bismo, San Forenso, Red Ante (where Bart mercifully kills Palto), San Pasquali, among others. And while Monte Vallejo himself never materializes, his Villaesque likeness is too significant not to be noted, much as Mexicali Burton seems derived from William Cornell Greene, holder of extensive cattle and mining operations in Sonora.

And while Comfort's Spanish is faulty, he does make an effort to flavor his story with bits of the language. Bart himself later is romantically fixed in his father's mind as the old man sketches his son for Elbert, and even Bart's mother is socially upgraded: "You know, Bart's mother was Spanish," he confides to Elbert, further painting his son as a splendid horseman, with "Spanish on his tongue, Mexican spurs and reata, more interested in guitar music than gold mining, and off by himself or with the Mexicans instead of with his own kind."

There even are instances seeking to depict the passing of the Old West, the cowboy, the once open range, to be found now only in "the fenceless foothills of Sonora." Indeed, it is only after another passage through the magic curtain that Elbert crosses the border near the Heaslep spread and looks up Cal and Slim who, weary of making forty dollars a month and certain they are "dyin' off here," decide to join him in his unrevealed mission, Elbert having sworn to the older Leadley to disclose to no one the object of his quest.

Further, even a reported train holdup at the San Isidro gorge by Vallejo and his men seems to be taken straight out of a similar incident pulled off by Villistas during Mexico's Revolutionary years. But then Comfort was a newsman. Born in Kalamazoo, Michigan, in 1878, he served in the Spanish-American War and later as a war correspondent in the Philippines, China, Russia and Japan. It was after that he hammered out a living as a novelist, producing a series of books from 1912 until his death at age fifty-four at his home in Los Angeles in 1932.

Although Comfort was best known for his novel *Routledge Rides Again,* whose graphic depictions of the horrors of war resulted in its being nominated for a Nobel prize (and its author reputedly winding up in a sanitarium after a fifty-day drunk following completion of the book), his 1925 novel *Somewhere South in Sonora* remains perhaps the exemplary border novel, a classic of the genre. Despite its drawbacks, it is the quintessential border tale of legendary adventure and romance on the vast stage that is encompassed by the magic curtain.

❦ ❦ ❦

While for Comfort, writing in the 1920s, very recent or almost contemporary happenings of the time formed much of the basis of *Somewhere South in Sonora,* the much longer arm of history is employed in *Fandango* by Ron McCoy, writing in the 1980s. Although billed as a Western, the novel is thoroughly dependent on the border; and once again, the area is familiar, the locale of Arizona and Sonora. The title itself is borderish, even though, as the author points out, the novel has nothing to do with the lively Spanish dance imported into the New World but rather "deals with the whirl as carried out in life." Certainly many of the typical border elements are present, including Mexican bandits, a buried treasure chest of loot, a genuine Mexican aristocrat fallen on hard times by yet another wholesale change of regime in his country, even romance blossoming on the other side of the magic curtain. But, there are also historical aspects treated that are less well known, particularly the shadowy and itinerant presence of Southern Confederates, and the brief heyday of steamboats plying the Colorado River.

The year is 1878. The place is the Arizona Territorial Prison, "hewn out of solid rock by its first fifteen inmates." It is near Yuma, twenty miles north of the Mexican border in the hot sprawl of harsh desert country.

Noteworthy among the prisoners are Ignacio Gomez, former Duke of Sonora, a title bestowed on him by Maximilian himself during the French-imported puppet emperor's 1864 to 1867 rule in Mexico, and Gomez's loyal retainer, Tino Mondragon. Although Gomez's titular position was on the whole as precarious as it was short-lived, for a time he had managed at least to hang on to his fragile empire, a hundred-mile strip of land along the Sea of Cortez that reached inland for ninety miles.

Gomez's duchy, a sizable holding by any reckoning, thus embraced several seaports—and, consequently, opportunities for profiteering from such ports of entry. In 1864, for example, Gomez had struck a deal with a cadre from the Confederate States: for the sum of $100,000 he would allow safe passage across his domain to 500 Confederate soldiers and embarkation from one of his ports. The financial transaction was to be made at Puerto Peligroso (Port Danger, a fitting appellation). Treachery was afoot; the four Confederate couriers were ambushed by an armed band of Juaristas (followers of Benito Juárez) on coming ashore. A lone Confederate survivor, soon to die, managed only to sketch vaguely for Gomez where he and his fallen comrades had buried a teakwood chest in which they had stashed the fortune, reputedly in gold.

Some three years later, the French had pulled out of Mexico, of course, and with Juárez triumphant the status of the stripped nobleman had changed drastically. Gomez and his faithful servant, Tino, a 350-pound colossus, swiftly decamped, sailing the ducal yacht to a safer clime in San Francisco. Meanwhile Gomez's treasury had been seized as compensation by United States officials for American citizens whose former holdings in Sonora Gomez himself earlier had appropriated. Although some $25,000 remained it had been deposited in an American bank at Tubac, Arizona Territory, near the Sonora border.

Eventually, almost penniless, Gomez lay plans to go to Tubac to obtain the funds, first stowing away on a clipper ship to San Pedro, then stealing a pair of horses at Los Angeles for the overland ride to Tubac. There, however, Gomez learns the sum has been impounded until such time as all American claims against him have been satisfied. Confronted with that sad news, he and Tino elect to take matters into their own hands, stealing the $25,000 and hightailing it toward the twin hamlets of Lado on the Arizona-Sonora border. There, Gomez visits old friend Sam Tong, originally of Shanghai and now owner of a saloon-restaurant-hotel in the American Lado. Tong barely has time to take possession of the stolen money before pursuing officers of the law arrive and cart Gomez and Tino off to prison.

Thus begins the pair's career of incarceration on a fifteen-year sentence. As the story opens they now have served eleven years—four years to go; yet, even upon their release from the territorial prison they still would be turned over to California authorities to face horse-theft charges there. Over the years it has been the sporadic doling out of the money guarded by Tong (less his twenty-three percent handling charges) that has enabled the diminutive Gomez and the massive Tino to survive with a few luxuries in the notoriously tough prison. Now, even that capital is nearly depleted, and more than ever they entertain the thought of escape. Some have tried and paid with their lives—if the desert fails to do them in, Indian bounty hunters will.

It is at that point that Sam Powers joins the inmates. A former marshal gone bad, Powers is there for a stay of about three months, when he will be hanged for having killed two sheriffs in a dispute over money. Powers then, a hardened case at age forty-four and now with nothing to lose but his life, is just the sort of man Gomez has been waiting for with whom to engineer a flight to freedom. To the renegade former law officer Gomez unfolds the story of the buried fortune, of which Powers will receive a substantial portion provided they escape.

That they manage to do, with Powers using his native cunning to throw their pursuers off their trail. Rather than head for the border, Powers has them flee north. Following the Colorado River they commandeer one of the vessels plying the formidable stream. Then, aboard the *Arizona Nile,* an eighty-foot paddlewheeler, they proceed to steam southward to the river's mouth in the Sea of Cortez.

The atmosphere of that hard and steamy countryside is evoked—the monotony and emptiness of the surrounding desert, the overpowering heat, the perception of impending change in crossing the imaginary line of the border and its magic curtain of escape. Gomez, suggests the narrator, believes he can feel the difference in the air itself. Eleven years away from his native land, he has already all but raised the curtain, even painting out the ship's name and painting in a Spanish one, *Fuego y Fuerte.*

Alas, the steamboat founders, gets hung up on a sandbar and dies soon afterward. Meanwhile, a bit of romance has developed between Powers and Kate McGuire, a young woman half his age. Niece of the captain of the now-wrecked vessel, the Santa Fe schoolteacher had been visiting her uncle and had chanced to be alone aboard the *Arizona Nile* at the time the escaped prisoners had stolen the craft. Luckily, Powers had had the foresight to provision the paddlewheeler with food and mules, with which they swim ashore. The magic curtain now has fully opened; they begin to make their way along the lonely Sonora coast, the old haunts of the former duke.

Raising the magic curtain, however, always enlarges the stage; now trouble awaits them stemming from both sides of the border. Shrike Jenkins, a professional scalp hunter who had escaped with the trio from the prison, has slipped away with some of the mules, made his way back to the border hamlet of Sonoyta and cut a deal with the garrison captain, José Redondo. Not only will Jenkins be able to collect the reward offered for Gomez, he also hopes to find Gomez's buried treasure and keep it all for himself.

Nearer to hand is the archetypal Mexican bandit Chaco, a likable ruffian who confronts Gomez and Powers and company and convinces them that Jenkins and Redondo, with a sizable force of troops, already are on their trail. On the strength of Chaco's argument they bow to the bandit's suggestion to team up with him, dig up the treasure together and all share in the spoils.

For that privilege Chaco will thus forego turning in Gomez for the much smaller reward. Chaco and his band join forces and they proceed toward Puerto Peligroso and the buried treasure. En route they sojourn briefly at the hamlet of Santa Rosalía, where a new romance develops, this time between Gomez and Nuria de Cordova, daughter of the local cantina owner, with Gomez vowing to return to her.

Moreover, Gomez, ever the optimist—no doubt reflective on his former grandeur and subject to the enchantment of the magic curtain of escape—has attempted to convince the bandit leader that the political situation might be changing. Gomez's star could rise again he suggests, urging Chaco and his men to become soldiers in what he envisions as his new army, advising the outlaw that such a career would be no different from the one they presently pursued. "Government," he informs the bandit, "is just banditry with paper and badges."

But if Gomez is temporarily deluded, enthralled in the enchantment of the opened magic curtain, he is soon dispossessed of his visionary return to grandeur. On arriving at Puerto Peligroso they find it a veritable ghost town. Gomez's former ducal mansion is only a ruin. Nothing is left with which the former duke might make a fresh start. However, they do find the teakwood chest of buried treasure. It is filled with Confederate money. Even as they unearth the box filled with the worthless currency, Jenkins arrives, prepared to wrest it away from them, but soon loses his life, stabbed to death by the ever faithful Tino.

Chaco and company, having no taste for the soldierly life suggested to them by Gomez, bid all farewell. Gomez himself will stay on in the area that once was his private fief, suggesting he soon will rendezvous with Nuria in Santa Rosalía. Powers, at last revealing his role in the affair, also makes ready to depart. His secret mission had been to reclaim the treasure for the United States government, his incarceration had been but a ruse in order to free Gomez so that he might win his confidence and lead him to the alleged cache of gold. Enough of spy work, he avers; he and the young schoolmarm will be heading back toward Santa Fe and a life together. Once more the magic curtain will be pulled to a final closing.

While *Fandango* is the prototypical modern Western, it is also the essential border novel, primed not only with escape from a bitterly harsh prison but also across the primal and legendary magic curtain of escape. Although fictional license of course is taken with some of the elements, on the whole McCoy hews to a line of historical accuracy, including numerous place names, the Arizona Territorial Prison, the short-lived and sometimes folly-ridden epoch of Colorado River steamboating, the rather chaotic state of affairs in Sonora. Indeed, McCoy, a graduate of Arizona State University, is a longtime student of the American Southwest and son of the renowned Hollywood western star Tim McCoy with whom he co-authored *Tim McCoy Remembers the West*.

A patina of historical authenticity thus genuinely flavors *Fandango,* including even a derived touch of transfused aristocracy emanating from the days of Maximilian and Carlota as emperor and empress of Mexico, in the character of Gomez, the fallen Duke of Sonora, and his once grand duchy along the Sea of Cortez. A touch of majesty is thus added to the grand realm of the magic curtain, even as escape by steamboat through the burnished desert countryside itself adds luster to the fabled domain of transformation and the grand escape. And while the buried treasure turns out to be as worthless as most tales of lost mines and buried treasure so legendary throughout the borderlands, and Chaco and his bandits prove to be not such a bad sort after all, the magic curtain is fully operative. Gomez and the faithful Tino can, like Alice through the famous looking glass, re-enter that from which they long ago had fled; and Powers and McGuire again can pass through the magic curtain toward a new life for both, on the other side.

Larry McMurtry's *Streets of Laredo* is not so much a true border novel as it is a novel about the border, the Texas border with Mexico. It can be pinpointed even further; in effect, the story's focus is the Texas border with Chihuahua and that looping area of the Rio Grande where it forms the Big Bend country. It is big country, bleak, and thinly settled. Border towns are few and far between.

Apart from the doleful cowboy ballad entitled *Streets of Laredo* (also known as *The Dying Cowboy*) that serves as the novel's title, the border town of Laredo is fairly removed from the center of the action, of which there is an astonishing amount, for McMurtry is a gifted storyteller. Threadbare lives are woven together with the deftness of a spider spinning its web, and, of course, the web of a spider is a death-trap.

Streets of Laredo is a novel about death. Figuratively speaking, it's a novel about the border as a pallbearer of death. Death emerges early on in the guise of Joey Garza, a nineteen-year-old Mexican recently embarked on a career of robbery and murder on the Texas side of the line. After all, that is where the money is, or what little there is in that area, and also gringos. Garza hates gringos in particular, and most other humans as well, and is much given to killing them at will. In short, Joey Garza is a very clever psychopath.

He is not the essential hybrid of so many border novels, but he does possess some of the usual traits. Already, and throughout the book, his given name is anglicized, and apparently he is fluent in English. Moreover, he is blond (a *güero,* as the Spanish language has it) and fair-skinned. The firstborn of María Garza, his mother, Joey Garza is a bad seed gone worse. He is a harbinger of death.

Not yet out of his teens, already he has killed numerous times and robbed seven trains. American trains. That, of course, has gained the rapt attention of railroad magnates Leland Stanford and Colonel Sheridan Terry. Consequently, Terry has hired the renowned Woodrow Call, the celebrated former Texas Ranger captain, to hunt down Garza. Because the famous manhunter's services are quite costly, Terry has sent down by train from New York his accountant Ned Brookshire to join the manhunt and keep a close watch on Call's expenses.

Brookshire is totally inept for such an assignment, about as fitted for a manhunt in the Texas wilderness as Call would be for bookkeeping chores in New York. However, two more men soon join up with Call to hunt Garza. They are Ted Plunkert, who is the Laredo deputy sheriff and Call's ever-loyal follower and former Ranger corporal whose apparently true name is Pea Eye. Given Call's advanced age, and the overriding preoccupation of his trio of followers for dealing with homesickness and the pangs of leaving their young wives, Call's makeshift posse is not one to inspire confidence that any of them will live long enough to hunt down Garza, known as a crack shot and possessor of a rifle with telescopic lens, a rarity at that time. Call's best defense lies in the fact that Garza does not know they are after him. That condition, however, shortly changes, and once Garza is aware of their mission, soon it is Garza who is hunting his pursuers.

For a while the volatile desperado has been holed up in Crow Town, a fictional community of depravity some 200 miles from the border in the sand hills of West Texas. Crow Town is an abominable place of whores, whiskey and unprincipled men, and lingering death. And it is to Crow Town that María Garza has traveled, all the way from poverty-stricken Ojinaga, the border town opposite Presidio, Texas, to warn her son that Captain Call is coming for him. For her trouble, her son steals her horse, thus forcing the mother that he hates above all others to return on foot and with no provisions in exceedingly harsh weather back across the 200 miles of barren country to Ojinaga.

To young Garza, all women are whores, among whom he includes his mother, who has had four husbands, all dead, and the second of whom sold Joey Garza as a slave to a band of Apaches. The young boy was with the Apaches for two years before he was able to escape. The episode obviously added to his self-hatred, and his self-hatred is inflicted on most all who cross his path.

María Garza's evil son with the cold killer's eyes is, in essence, a sort of conglomerate of Mexican stereotype in the preoccupation with death, cuckoldry, insane sexual jealousy, and the tawdry glamour associated with border balladry, and legendary antiheroes destined to die young, as does the "done wrong" cowboy in the *Laredo* ballad. Joey Garza's fate is also sealed, but there is much more havoc, mayhem and murder before he goes.

McMurtry's predilection for ultimate violence is excessive, even in this horse-opera saga of the Old West. Lurking in the background, for example, for Call and others to deal with is the personification of evil in the character Mox Mox the man burner and his gang of seven. Mox Mox particularly delights in burning alive young children. All told, there is enough killing, blood and gore for two or three novels, and enough dwelling on the grim and empty lives of post-frontier survivors to make *Streets of Laredo* an exercise in clinical depression. Though billed as a sequel to McMurtry's *Lonesome Dove, Streets of Laredo* stands comfortably on its own as a border novel. It is populated with enough historical personages to make the fictional characters seem genuinely authentic in the intertwining of their harsh and lonely lives. Women die off, men are killed, or hopelessly maimed for life.

The border country itself is king, epitomized by the dual towns of Ojinaga and Presidio; but it is a land of sorrow, desperation, emptiness. It is a vale of tears and oppression, of lost spirits and little hope. So little hope is there that in the homicidal career of Joey Garza there is a grim logic in his persistence as an angel of death bent on wiping out the primal roots of his own existence.

10

Through the Looking Glass of the Hybrid Culture

In the literature of the border it is not that the area itself stamps some geographical change on its characters; rather it is the divisiveness of the boundary which becomes of paramount importance. And so it is in meeting the challenge of its two cultures that the artistry of such novelists must come into play. The boundary, the vast border country alone, becomes the canvas on which such tales are painted, and the tellers of them must draw on that heritage, interpreting a hybrid people and a harsh land.

The classic example in the field, however, regards it in a far more romanticized manner. For Tom Lea the tough land becomes instead *The Wonderful Country*, and the novel has as much to do with northern Mexico as with the American Southwest. In its unfolding of a period of actually less than a year in the life of the heroic protagonist Martin Brady, Lea is forced into accounting for Brady's earlier life. And for Brady, more than half of that, some fourteen years, has been spent in the north of the Mexican republic.

Consequently a great deal of Brady's exotic past must be disposed of before he can emerge as a full-blown American—indeed, as a Texas Ranger. And, as in any sort of intercultural transition or rebirth, the transformation is traumatic: If much is gained, much, too, is lost. Correspondingly, a large share of tragedy ensues before Martín Bredy—the Hispanicized version of his name he long has answered to as a vaquero on the immense Valdepeñas hacienda—can be reshaped into Martin Brady, a bona fide Texas American and an invaluable addition to the Texans' extraterritorial police force because of his hybrid cultural background, an ability to understand both sides, to be equally at home in either cultural situation.

In Brady's case, his transition is not even complicated by an alien birth. Like most protagonists of border literature, Brady is fully pedigreed, having fled to Mexico as a youth after he had "used his father's pistol on his father's killer." An understated if unsung plea for justifiable homicide is thus implanted early on.

Divided loyalties, occasioned in many instances of crossbreeding or interracial marriages and so forth, are not the real cause of concern to Brady. There isn't any conflict arising from "miscegenation," and in that *The Wonderful Country* avoids the stylization of frustration and alienation centered in the progeny of such unions. It is instead Brady's dual acculturation, his identification with both peoples who are guardedly separated by the institution of the boundary, the magic curtain, which is the basis for this confusion. It is a necessary outgrowth of both sentiment and training derived from his habits of long association through years of residence among both peoples, and at Brady's age now it is an evenhanded sixteen.

It has made of him the classic hybrid and the very personification of the split personality shaped by biculturalism. Because of that he comes into his disrupted American heritage only gradually and only after several further misadventures, extenuating contacts with a number of persons who had been so much and for so very long a part of his life, as well as his coming of age, in the sprawling north of Mexico, principally Chihuahua, where the

Castro brothers, Cipriano, the elder and administrator of their enterprises, and Marcos, an army general, run the state.

His acquired roots run deep. So much so that it first appears that he cannot accomplish so difficult a transition. Not only is there the abiding anxiety he has of facing eventual punishment for the slaying of his father's killer, but later, in trying to come in for and live up to his mature Americanization process, he is once more compelled to retreat across the border for having done away with yet another man on United States soil.

It might seem that the die has been cast long ago and that Brady cannot escape the web of his past. He will resume his former career as chief gunfighter in the service of the wealthy hacendado Castro, his employer-benefactor, in short, his patrón. Unknown to Brady, however, is the fact that Brady's latter victim had been a criminal with a reward posted for him, dead or alive.

But the magic curtain, in novels as in life, is always miraculous, even if it is late in coming. Thus, only after further picaresque events is Brady made aware that he has been freed of criminal charges in both deaths. The slate is now clean, and the past can even be profitable. In the case of Brady he is permitted to enlist in the Rangers. Moreover, in an ensuing excursion into Mexico with the Rangers in pursuit of Apaches, Brady is forced into relinquishing his most intimate tie with his Mexican past. His formidable Andalusian-bred horse Lágrimas (Tears), a momentous and superlative gift from his longtime boss and latent surrogate father Cipriano Castro, is purposely shot by an old foe, Abrán Rascón.

In an age in which killing a man's horse was almost equivalent to wiping out a member of the family, or in some instances perhaps even more despicable, Brady retaliates, avenging the slaying of Lágrimas by dispatching Rascón. Rather than a border romance, *The Wonderful Country* substitutes a thoroughgoing equestrian affair. Which is proper in the novel's placement in border literature and the magic curtain of escape, on horseback generally and only later in motorized traffic, airplane, even ship (as in

Ron McCoy's *Fandango*). After all, the magic curtain is freedom, and a valiant steed most effectively exemplifies it.

And so the time is ripe for Brady to erase the last vestige of his colorful if unlawful past, leaving all the trappings on Lágrimas—even his saddlebags, "everything," summarizes Brady, "I had in Mexico." As the force of Rangers moves north, back toward the Rio Grande, the Great River, ever the symbol of the other America, the re-Americanization of Martin Brady is complete.

❦ ❦ ❦

Equally faithful in depicting the region of the border and those who have come under its unshakable influence are a pair of novels by the Texas folklorist Frank Goodwyn. But the themes of both of Goodwyn's contributions to border literature, *The Magic of Limping John* and *The Black Bull,* are diametrically opposed to Lea's exemplary tale.

Rather than utilizing an American long resident in Mexico as protagonist, both of Goodwyn's novels are centered around Mexican Americans long resident in the United States, specifically the near border country of southern Texas. In both there is thus no need for reaching south of the border to effect an exotic backdrop. Rather, that exoticism has been carried forward inherently by the characters themselves, not only the protagonists but lesser characters within their circle of influence. All of them, in fact, have been dropped seemingly pell mell into the American milieu, a culture more forced upon them than sought, and thus one in which they exist but do not truly live.

In Goodwyn's earlier novel, *The Magic of Limping John,* the community itself, the hamlet of Los Puentes (The Bridges) is unshakably Mexicanized, and its most popular institution is the local cantina, El Caballo Negro (the Black Horse saloon). Los Puentes is a village of stark simplicity and economic leanness to the point of near paucity. Thus it plays out its rather moribund though measured life in the rituals of births and deaths, weddings and christenings and occasionally successful seductions with little more than intermittent fiestas and a few bottles of tequila to relieve the monotony of it all.

It is in such a locale that Limping John Luna (here, too, the patronym is significant, *luna* being the Spanish word for moon) ekes out a living with his violin, performing at such village festivities where musical entertainment is called for. The story itself might best be summarized as the waxing and waning of the fiddler who, in the carefully graded social strata of Los Puentes, ultimately is propelled into the affluent and commanding position of village wizard, an occupation not so much sought by Juan de Luna, to use his true Spanish name, as forced upon him by his fellow citizens.

Limping John, a thoroughgoing individualist, is also what would be termed a freethinker in the world of catechismal Christendom evinced in the superstition-ridden village of Los Puentes. On the strength of such outspoken heresy and certain later bizarre happenings in which the musician appears to have had a hand, local gossips at once perceive a connection between those uncanny events and the mysterious, solitary, bachelor ways of the bearded fiddler with the strong face and limping gait.

For the well-known figure to protest is but to fire their imaginations and instill their beliefs all the more, and so almost overnight Juan de Luna is elevated to the role of *curandero,* or village healer. At once he begins to be paid quite substantial sums not only, in that dualistic world of black and white, fair and foul, to exercise his powers of good but correspondingly to desist from calling into play his presumed powers of evil. Limping John can have it both ways: At once there comes about for the humble fiddle player a respect he has never known, riches he has scarcely dared to dream of.

Fundamentally, *The Magic of Limping John* is a bicultural allegory in which freedom, as proscribed by the magic curtain of the border, is lost by the very pitfalls occasioned in a transplanted heritage—the Mexicanized past seeking to operate still in an out-of-the-way pocket of the American culture. It is both allegory and dilemma: One must always pay the fiddler; and the fiddler himself must also pay in crossing the magic curtain of escape.

The underlying philosophy is exhibited early in the novel by means of a tale related by one of Limping John's confederates, Fabian Balboa. The story concerns Christ and the Devil, both of whom "while walking across the world" one day chanced to observe a cow drinking at a waterhole.

Christ, urged by the Devil to demonstrate his power and cause the beast to become stuck, readily obliges. Shortly a cowboy happens by, tries to free the animal and blames the cow's predicament on the Devil. Immediately the Devil uses his own power to retrieve the cow from the mud. Forthwith the cowboy praises the Lord for effecting its rescue.

"A man," concludes Fabian, "is made of what people think about him."

The anecdote pithily symbolizes the case, and fate, of Limping John himself. At first averse to accepting the villagers' beliefs about him, John finally becomes convinced that his fellow citizens are correct in their estimation of him—that he truly does have the powers of a wizard and healer. It has been manifested to him not only materially but in the towering rise of the esteem in which they hold him; his prestige has soared to the point of near enshrinement.

In short, the ne'er-do-well fiddler has made tremendous gains, but in so doing he has lost not only the liberty of his freethinking ways but also his freedom itself. As a captive of illusions—others' as well as his own—Limping John finds he has paid an unconscionable price. In his encompassing frustration he at last smashes his beloved fiddle in a fit of desperation while playing at his own wedding. The ultimate holdout is finally about to be embraced by the cultural rituals in which he long had been more functionary than participant, a part of the magic curtain himself rather than one of its escapees.

Like *The Magic of Limping John* the setting of *The Black Bull* is also the southern tip of Texas. Its characters, too, are Mexican—if not in nationality, at least in all other respects—undergoing a superficial process in nominal Americanization. Indeed, it becomes the mission of Goodwyn in both novels to portray persistent Mexicanization in the face of overwhelming Americanization, not only through political allegiance, technology and economics but through birthright as well. It becomes the focal point of both works to dwell on the carrying over of virtually antiquated customs of Mexico in order to make a case for the slow stagnating acculturation process and, ergo, ongoing exoticism. Both novels, in that sense are tales of a people who not only cannot relinquish their folkways but rather continue to embrace them, nurture them. Those, in fact, are the sole quality that gives a wholeness to their being, renders some meaning to their fragile existence, which already is being steadily squeezed to death by an alien Anglo clime.

The locale for *The Black Bull* is the brush country of southern Texas where "things of eternity prevail." With a few strokes Goodwyn paints the environment of heat and aridity, dry winds and prickly pear. It is, in essence, an imagery more north Mexican than American. And, for all practical purposes, it truly is a transplanted piece of Mexico rather than of Texas or the United States. Its characters are, in effect, a part of the changeless, hard-bitten land and the deeply rooted folklike conservatism that so often have passed as the pictorial image for all of Mexico.

The theme of *The Black Bull* is concerned with the life (and early death) of Robelín Alegría, a young man who had come up from Mexico to work on the large ranch known as the Candelaria and who now has been in the United States for about a decade. The vast Candelaria (like the immense and world-renowned King Ranch of South Texas) is divided into numerous ranchos. Such subdivisions of the cattle empire themselves still bear Mexican names (the Tenerías, the Tecolote) and are commonly supervised by highly respected individuals of Mexican or even Spanish lineage, as exemplified by the book-loving, guitar-playing Agustín Mendoza, the bachelor caretaker of the Zanahoria rancho.

Thus the Candelaria is essentially a hacienda, operating just as have such vast landed estates of northern Mexico for some three centuries. The Candelaria in particular remains a tenuous network of ranchos on which the workers lead something of a communal-like existence, tied together by their common workaday life, and, on the Candelaria in particular, by their habits of life which have been transplanted from greater Mexico.

The rancho communities are dominated by the Candelaria-built homes for the married ranch hands. Those, of course, are a cut above the more spartan quarters for unmarried workers, such as Robelín, and an even more recent émigré from Mexico named Eugenio Barrientes. Both, as escapees across the magic curtain, have sought the better life in the United States, have found a home for their ranchero talents on the Candelaria, so Mexicanized that the two easily fit in with its overall operation.

The work on the great ranch itself goes forward by grouping the men into *corridas*. As members of Corrida Number Two, both Robelín and Eugenio work daily with Timoteo Niveto. As straw-boss for their particular corrida, Timoteo is also appropriately their elder, and thus their mentor. Don Timoteo, as he is respectfully addressed, is a master vaquero, fittingly wise by virtue of both his years and hard life. He is also the father of a strikingly beautiful daughter, Josefa, whom both Robelín and Eugenio have in mind to wed, even though the latecomer Eugenio has yet to reveal his matrimonial aims. Conflict lies in the fact that Robelín, to whom Josefa has given the nod of approval, is quite disturbed by such a commitment and openly rebellious at the idea of marriage.

The tale runs its course quite smoothly. As in the case of

Limping John, the story is devoted to portraying the undoing of Robelín. One day, while the men are engaged in running a herd of cattle into pens for ensuring shipment to market by rail, a powerful, seven-year-old bull, forebodingly black, leaps out of the chute. Robelín and Eugenio, already duly famous as two of the best ropers on the whole Candelaria, are immediately dispatched to catch the runaway. Their mission turns out to be a far more serious and dangerous a business than might be supposed. So much so that eventually the entire force of Corrida Number Two becomes occupied in that singularly hazardous affair. While for most of the vaqueros it is little more than a part of the workaday routine, for Robelín it becomes a consuming passion and his chief purpose in life. Robelín's quest is intensified after the runaway bull gores and tramples to death the venerable Agustín, and it is only after long hard days of arduous tracking and harassing the black beast that Robelín succeeds in capturing it.

Having accomplished that, Robelín, a taciturn, moody and hopelessly serious young man, decides to release the black bull so that it might be free once more. On doing so the bull instantly attacks its benefactor's horse, then Robelín himself, killing them both. Subsurfacely, too, something else has been symbolically lost: Happiness, which is Robelín's last name, Alegría, when translated into English.

With Robelín thus out of the way for good, Josefa and Eugenio ultimately are wed and forthwith embark on having a family. The reader is left with fair justification to assume that Eugenio will follow in the sober footsteps of his young wife's father, leading the simple life, working hard and leaving a large progeny.

Eugenio has made good his escape across the magic curtain, whereas Robelín, seeker of a greater freedom, has attained that, too, despite his leaving little more than a memory and the bootless story of his empty life. Escape across the magic curtain has quite swallowed him up, even though the downfall of the protagonists in both Goodwyn novels has been brought about by conflicts and disturbances in their own characters rather than by some cultural conflict. Moreover, such flaws have arisen out of their heritage, which is Mexican, not Anglo, a heritage which quite simply has been only transplanted on the other side of the magic curtain comprised by the border.

There is perhaps a deeper symbolism at work as well here in the union of Josefa and Eugenio: Josefa, the daughter of Don Timoteo, highly successful and respected member of the working class, and Eugenio, his appropriate successor, fusing new blood from Mexico into a now-established American lineage. The older ancestry, that of the dispossessed landed aristocracy exemplified by the melancholy and quasi-intellectual Agustín, is effectively ended in his own bachelorhood, while the confused idealist Robelín has been nobly damned from the outset. As in life itself, the magic curtain giveth, and the magic curtain also taketh away.

Adding to this particular area of border literature is the Chicano fiction of Rolando Hinojosa, author of several works set in mythical Belken County in the lower Rio Grande Valley, and especially the town of Klail City, the county seat. The fictionalized locale closely resembles that of Hidalgo County, Texas, where Hinojosa was born in 1929.

The entire output is conceived as a single chronicle of what the author calls the Klail City Death Trip Series. As a whole, the books seek to convey the changing culture and lifestyles of "borderers" in the increasingly mixed world of Anglos and Hispanics. Indeed, some of the books have English as well as Spanish versions. The books are rather brief, experimental in format, decidedly out of mainstream publishing, and fraught with editorial oversights.

Within the series, only *Partners in Crime*, which follows a reasonably conventional mystery story format, merits consideration as a border novel. It is a rather untidy tale whose action spills across the river into Mexico, as cocaine dealers seek to take over the less profitable marijuana market, unleashing the usual violence and corruption.

In essence, a multiple homicide has occurred in Belken County—a local resident and two Mexican nationals. The three have been killed at the Kum-Bak Inn, a motel and watering hole a few miles outside Klail City. No connection, however, seems to exist between the two Mexicans and the local man; Gustave Ambrose (Dutch) Elder simply had happened upon something he should not have seen. Inasmuch as the murders constitute an international incident, a Mexican official, Lisandro Gómez Solís, is brought in to work the case. A captain in the Tamaulipas state police unit at mythical Barrones just across the boundary, he is the Mexican counterpart of Rafe Buenrostro, a lieutenant in the Belken County homicide squad assigned to the case.

Luckily, the amiable captain speaks flawless English; it so happens that he is a graduate of the University of Illinois (from which the author himself earned a doctoral degree). He is also a fount of information and well apprised of the usual border activities within his purview: smuggling, killings, auto thefts, and bank irregularities. Gómez, in fact, for years has been aware of marijuana smuggling by a group of Klail City women. He let it go on because, he claims, keeping tabs on such shipments led the police to larger cargoes of contraband.

The women were unwitting accomplices. It was their custom to gather each Sunday in Barrones to dine and later drive back across the border to play canasta. Unbeknownst to the canasta players, while their several cars were parked, bricks of marijuana were placed beneath the fenders. Respectable, long-time Klail City residents all, the women were never stopped for border searches. Later, traffickers in the trade would collect the stashes of mota from each of the cars.

Obviously, Gómez and his associates had learned particulars

about the canasta-playing women—names, addresses, makes of their cars and the license plates. Thus, when the car of Mrs. Laura Sikes, one of the principal players, is found missing, a number of questions are raised. Some of those relate to certain coincidences noted by Gómez Solís himself, which, on second thought, seem far too coincidental to have been mere happenstance. Sorting them out is a complex and tedious affair, and even at book's end there are still some unsettled details and innuendoes strewn about.

Partners in Crime (billed as a Rafe Buenrostro Mystery) is not a smoothly flowing story. The plot is impeded by a plethora of trivia not germane to the tale, and the reader is introduced to far too many characters who have little depth and even less memorability. Inconsequential detail is furnished where facts would be helpful, and tag words at the end of dialogues and elsewhere read like stage directions in an unfinished playscript.

As in so much of the Klail City Death Trip Series, there seems more a concerted effort to reveal certain Klail City secrets and obscure personages than to entertain readers not familiar with such an environment. *Partners in Crime* is, notwithstanding its murder mystery genre, in its way about as gossipy as most of the other books in the series, reflecting small-town mores as well as an oral tradition in storytelling. And though the novel reflects at least some of the social change that has taken place in border communities, little is depicted in maturity and growth of this cultural transformation. There are no philosophical insights, no sweeping observations. It's a young person's story.

There is, for example, a sort of sophomoric crudity in the overtly sexualized spelling of the Kum-Bak Inn, a place that, by dint of it being the scene of the killings, must be referred to frequently. There is also something of the "in" joke sort of meaning to the surnames of Rafe Buenrostro and his cousin and friend Jehú Malacara—literally the Goodface and Badface of the two men, both now in their thirties, who were orphans during the

Great Depression years of the 1930s. Perhaps they function as ego and alter ego of the author, for their stories unfold in bits and pieces throughout the series.

Sympathy favors the good Buenrostro, a widower at the tender age of nineteen after his young wife drowned during a picnic on the Rio Grande, and later a lawyer who has waived a legal career in favor of becoming a police officer. Not so congenial is the bad Malacara, a loan officer at one of Klail City's three banks, believed by some to be an embezzler.

Partners in Crime displays the cohesiveness of border communities as well as the depth of their insularity. But the sense of remoteness is always there, even as the two cultures become less segregated, not so profoundly isolated from one another in the nursing of ethnic differences that would distinguish, say, "Texas Mexicans" from Mexican Mexicans and from Anglos in general. Exemplary in that sense is the "Texano Mexicano" car thief José Francisco (Packy) de Paula Estudillo. Packy Estudillo is the first-class professional car thief who has stolen Laura Sikes' automobile. It is a theft he will regret very much, inasmuch as Estudillo is only a car thief and knew nothing about the use of her car for transporting marijuana each week. Nor is it sheer coincidence that Captain Gómez knew of the theft well before Buenrostro and others in his homicide unit knew of it. It is, however, the opportunity for the captain to explain about the 276 pounds of cocaine he has mentioned.

Smuggling, as old as the border itself, is no longer the sort of penny-ante operation it used to be. The 120 kilos of cocaine could be worth as much as seventy million American dollars. In short, *Partners in Crime* well establishes the fact that the border has become a place of big bucks. There is no glamour in all of this, nor romance, nor exoticism. The border is a cold and seedy place, full of temptation, and rife with corruption and insatiable greed.

At the end, when readers learn of some of the changes that have recently taken place in Barrones, a few things seem to fall into place. Gómez Solís, for example, is on vacation, having put in for medical retirement. The Lone Star restaurant, owned by the Gómez Solís family, where the unsuspecting canasta players habitually dined each Sunday evening, has been sold. And one of the younger Gómez Solís family members is allegedly managing the family's (no doubt now sizable) business interests just down the coast in the balmy Gulf port city of Tampico.

As one of Buenrostro's colleagues notes, 276 pounds of cocaine goes a long way. And so it does. Greed and corruption have a way of rubbing off on the innocent as well as the guilty and the unwary, unwitting dupes of a broader evil. Avarice is boundless—borderless—in creating unsuspecting helpmates in crime.

11

Wading Into the American Dream

A more embittered view of the boundary and the problems created by the international bureaucracy are to be found in yet another pair of novels: *White Shadows* by Guy Nunn, and Claud Garner's *Wetback*.

Both Nunn and Garner are deeply concerned with the tortuous chain of difficulties, the virtually endless and humiliating vexations with which Mexican émigrés have been saddled. As American spokesmen for such underdogs, their tales, accordingly, are stories of utter hardship, desperation, and gross exploitation, and they depict with painful progression the movement toward Americanization of their central characters, which only in the final analysis seems partially attainable. Even then it is less a matter of certainty than of abiding hope and cheerful predisposition.

White Shadows unfolds the story of the Alfierro family, from the Mexican west coast state of Jalisco. Pablo Alfierro, having dared to speak out against the practice in which ownership of land goes not to the people who work it but rather to an absentee gentry, soon finds his own small farm destroyed by those he had offended in his denunciation of but one aspect of an unjust system.

Wiped out, Pablo and his wife Josefina and their three children, rather than try to begin anew in so hypocritical and dangerous an environment, set out for the United States via Ciudad Juárez and El Paso. Having made their way that far, the usual hopeless situation arises with the immigration authorities. A paper bureaucracy guards the very prize that they can see, lying just beyond the international bridge across the renowned river. Nor does it, the bureaucratic guardians of vested interests, look kindly upon the likes of the poverty-stricken Alfierros.

Abjectly frustrated at being denied even a taste of their tantalizing goal, Pablo covertly crosses his family onto United States soil at an unguarded spot along the Great River. It is momentary success, but of a very dubious nature. Culture shock at once engulfs them. They are relentlessly bewildered by the foreignness of metropolitan El Paso, a city utterly different from anything they have ever known, and yet a place separated from their small familiar world only by a river.

Were it not for an uncle of Pablo long resident in El Paso, the situation for the Alfierros might well be beyond hope. The uncle, Lombardo Monteverde, a romantic bachelor with a philosophical bent, at once comes to their aid, assisting the Jaliscan family in finding a place to live and, perhaps equally importantly, conveying to them two fundamental lessons about their chosen country. Skin is nationality, Lombardo tells his newly arrived kinfolk, later adding lesson two: The sternest sort of humility, he informs them, must be practiced at all times in the presence of gringos.

As a result of practicing well Lombardo's advice, Pablo is soon successful in securing work through the clandestine but customary practice of contacting an *enganchador,* one of the illicit labor brokers who make a parasitic living by contracting out illegal aliens such as Pablo to work for ridiculously low wages. Pablo is immediately assigned to work on one of the slag heaps of the many smelters on the outskirts of the border city. A dehumanizing type of labor, the work further humbles Pablo by his being forced to work at so low a pay scale that it quickly breeds an intolerable situation for him in trying to make ends meet.

While Lombardo has become reasonably inured to such practices over the years, for the Alfierros the magic curtain that once glittered before their eyes has become tarnished almost overnight. Pablo, seeking any improvement in his employment condition, soon attempts to join a labor movement, whereupon he is seized, along with others in the unionizing effort, beaten and jailed.

Later freed, but narrowly escaping further detention as an illegal, Pablo deems it unwise to remain longer in El Paso. Forthwith, the Alfierro family, now including Lombardo—whose own working life always has left much to be desired and in teaming up with Pablo feels he has nothing left to lose—contract with another *enganchador*, signing on as migrant workers for the California harvests.

That way out of their predicament is also paved with despair, degeneration and, finally, the inevitable cessation of even that lowly paid work. Ultimately the family is driven to seek refuge and the hope of some means to a livelihood in the Spanish-speaking ghettos of Los Angeles. But there, too, work is anything but easy to come by, and what there is of it is just as poorly paid.

Their existence is no less precarious than before. Later, as the Depression years of the 1930s carve even deeper into the economy, further eroding the family's slender hold on dignity, Pablo remains jobless for months on end and times are difficult even for Lombardo, a skilled stonemason. Only after several years of penury does the situation of the Alfierro family improve. Pablo obtains a job of some stability as a machinist and embarks on the tenuous process of legalizing his entry into the United States, finally obtaining his coveted citizenship.

Meanwhile the Alfierro children have nearly reached maturity and are ready to embark on their own careers. Soon after the outbreak of World War II, the eldest son, Pepe, enlists in the army, and is later killed in Italy. The younger, Miguel, becomes a flier, and the daughter, Martita, soon becomes the betrothed of a young Anglo named Smith, one of her brother's friends at flight training school.

Even the dedicated bachelor uncle, Lombardo, finally succumbs to intercultural destiny, marrying an American widow, Mrs. Adams. And Pablo Alfierro himself has found an outlet for his own social passions as a staunch member of the *Congreso,* the burgeoning CIO (Congress of Industrial Organizations), the centralized federation of unions that had split off from the AFL (American Federation of Labor) in 1935.

If *White Shadows* is not the march triumphant of the American Dream, then it is very close to it, and the magic curtain is more than ever in place. Indeed, the magic curtain falls on idealism wholly realized. Lombardo, whose name is to be borne by the offspring of Martita, expresses the sentiment in a final toast: "Despite sixty and more years of experience to the contrary, I have suddenly discovered that the world is good. . . . Today a gringo called me 'Mister' and is my friend. But the best is that today I have been assured that my name will be borne through yet another generation, in a blend of the noblest of two noble races. . . . Gentlemen, we will drink to Mr. Lombardo Smith!"

For the Alfierros of *White Shadows,* virtue has been rewarded, all hardships overcome. Life on the other side of the magic curtain is the dream come true. Moreover, it has not destroyed one's roots but instead blended them into that ideal of a classless America and a New World of ungraded men and women.

Equally victorious in overcoming the snares, pitfalls and obstacles strewn in the pathway across the magic curtain is the enterprising hero of *Wetback,* Dionisio Jesús Molina. Although younger than Pablo Alfierro and not burdened with the responsibility of a family, Dionisio also has found life in Mexico exceedingly difficult. Disinherited by his mother's people, Tarascan Indians of the Uruápan area of Michoacán, because of her affair with a gringo prospector, Dionisio at age eighteen already has long made his own way in the world, principally as a guide for tourists in the city of Guadalajara.

The die is cast early on for this hybrid offspring and blending of the two cultures across the magic curtain. Even though never having known his own father, Dionisio so much resembles his tall, red-haired father that Dionisio's very presence has become a constant and painful reminder to his Indian mother of her early "disgrace." Thus acutely aware of the conflicting emotion he produced in his own mother, Dionisio has left home, striking out on his own at age thirteen.

Frugal and spartan in his habits of expenditure, he has saved his earnings during the ensuing five years of his picaresque existence. At last he has made so bold as to undertake the long journey up to Matamoros, with the view of crossing the magic curtain of the border via Brownsville, Matamoros' twin American city, and seeking his fortune in the foreign land of his father, the country of free enterprise, self-help and opportunity. But, like Pablo Alfierro, Dionisio Molina also has failed to reckon with the nightmare network of immigration officialdom. Naiveté and hope are soon beaten down by the costly, time-consuming and illogical battering rams of paperwork, pedigrees and personal credentials, affairs so vital in bureaus of immigration that it is as if the sole acquisition of those proofs of existence might be the ultimate purpose of life.

Frustrated to the point of desperation by the unreality of such paper tigers guarding the gates to his now-so-near goal, Dionisio, like the Alfierros, decides to enter the United States illegally, wading the river in the dead of night and emerging as a *mojado,* a wetback, on the other side. Crossing the magic curtain is at once both his salvation and his curse. Immediately he falls into that life of constant fear and continuous exploitation suffered by illegal aliens in any land. Notwithstanding his anxiety and utter alienation, Dionisio soon finds work as a laborer in a camp of workers clearing brushland. Wetbacks like himself, the workers are ruthlessly taken advantage of by the foreman, an American of Mexican heritage who, in the pecking order of exploitation, has surpassed his teachers in the practice of extortion, graft and vindictiveness.

Despite such an exploitive environment, Dionisio manages to save a part of his low pay as a means of escaping to a different, perhaps better, life. That aim is laid waste, however, when his savings are stolen by a camp follower, a woman of loose virtue who has the run of the place. Even that irreparable loss seems minor, however, when Dionisio and numerous others are dispatched for forcible return to Mexico following a "surprise" inspection of the camp by the Border Patrol. Unable to produce proper papers for being in the United States, the candidates for expulsion can be hurriedly rounded up, even beaten out of the latest pay due them. It is an event that will be revisited upon Dionisio several more times during his American hegira, the victim of unscrupulous employers who have succeeded in cashing in on an endless source of almost free labor.

It is only through the happenstance obtaining of a friend, Buck Hagan, that Dionisio is finally able to add some degree of stability to his precarious life. Hagan, a cattleman who is in the habit of pasturing a large part of his herd in Mexico, then selling them in the United States without benefit of any customs duties, unfolds a plan whereby their friendship can be mutually beneficial if they concentrate on raising a large flock of goats that Dionisio himself can take care of. Anxious to help his young charge as well as to protect his business venture, Hagan even secures forged papers for Dionisio so that he may avoid further fear, harassment and possible deportation.

With Hagan's help, Dionisio prospers, marries Rosita Cavazos, daughter of one of the old Hispanic families long resident in the lower Rio Grande Valley. The newlyweds even build themselves a house. And thus, having reached a new plateau in his young life, Dionisio and Hagan terminate their business arrangement on good terms. Things are looking up. Dionisio and Rosita, utilizing their savings, are even able to salvage what is left of her father's land which has not yet been filched for nonpayment of taxes. Later, following the death of Rosita's father, Dionisio puts the land into farming, and on a paying basis.

But the past is never a dead thing. One day Dionisio is summoned to face charges over his transactions with Hagan, who at last has been prosecuted for his nefarious cattle dealings. Dionisio, having had no part in that, is exonerated; however, the matter of his illegal status is brought out in the course of the trial. Only after further litigation is he permitted to return to Mexico with the express purpose of securing such necessary documents as will permit him to remain in the United States and lay claim to citizenship on the grounds of proving his father's American nationality.

Fittingly, that mission Dionisio accomplishes alone. After all, it is only he who has passed through the magic curtain, and now must do so again in order to prove, as it were, his own reality. But now he reenters the land of his birth as a virtual foreigner with his acquired English tongue, his American habits of dress, of conduct, attitude, even his American-made car. Swiftly and solitarily he makes his way back to Uruápan, deep in the interior of the Mexican republic, which now holds for him only dimming childhood memories—and now, more than ever, the passport to his future.

Dionisio secures the necessary credentials, even seeks out his mother, only to learn that she long since has married and moved yet farther south. Dionisio does not pursue the search. Quickly he returns to the border where he at once contacts a lawyer and has his papers put in order for making his legal entry into the country of his choice. His final Americanization is at hand as the attorney complies with Dionisio's request: that the lawyer drive Dionisio's car across the bridge so that he, Dionisio, may walk across and into his adopted homeland, the United States of America, with his head held high and eyes shining.

Like Martin Brady in *The Wonderful Country*, what Dionisio

Molina has left behind on the other side of the magic curtain is another self, only remnants of which will follow him now in his new—and thoroughly legal—life. It is a symbolic metamorphosis, as with the Alfierros of *White Shadows,* who, too, have become only shades of their former selves. Only the border, the epicenter of continuing cultural conflict, can raise or lower the curtain for the magicality in the baptism of rebirth.

❦ ❦ ❦

The romanticized image of the wetback lives on. Laurance L. Priddy's *Son of Durango*, published in 1996, continues the tradition. By now, however, the undercurrents of violence and crime have become so dominant that one's illegal immigrant status seems relatively minor. Drugs and prostitution are almost an institutional presence, and thus hazards of particular importance for anyone already living the life of an undocumented alien.

Consequently, just about everything that is bad happens to Jesus Camacho, a native of a small and unnamed village in Durango, the northwest central state just below the border state of Chihuahua. As we pick up his story, Jesus has recently crossed the border at Laredo. Now an illegal immigrant in the United States, he stealthily makes his way to Bandera in the central Texas Hill Country. His ultimate destination is the J. B. Tackett ranch, which is near Bandera and from which Jesus' younger brother Miguel has last written to him.

On arriving at the ranch, however, Jesus learns that Miguel has in the meanwhile gone to seek higher-paying work in Fort Worth, nearly three hundred miles to the north. Distraught after not finding his brother at the ranch, Jesus is allowed by Tackett to spend the night and, a couple of days later, permitted to stay on at the ranch and work. Anxious to continue his search for Miguel, but broke and trail weary, Jesus begins to work for Tackett, planning to continue looking for Miguel after he has saved enough money to travel to Fort Worth.

It is early established that Jesus is short on patience and seemingly has some sort of learned capacity for doing the wrong thing. One is getting drunk; another is misreading the look of Tackett's teen-age daughter and kissing her. When daughter Ellie reports this to her father, Jesus is forced to flee in disgrace, and with very little money to get to Fort Worth.

Errors on the part of Jesus are compounded thereafter. Fate seems to have laid a heavy hand on Jesus who, with an unerring propensity for bad judgment, seems destined to court failure. Even when things appear to be going relatively well, Jesus is bent on undermining any possibility of success. In Fort Worth, though he fails to find Miguel, he does encounter his own impending nemesis, Ernesto Caballero. Soon Jesus finds work at the Celestial Mobile Home factory and learns that Miguel earlier worked there but is told Miguel recently was arrested and deported. Shortly thereafter, Jesus himself narrowly escapes arrest in a sting operation carried out by a black policewoman when Jesus, believing her to be a prostitute, is attempting to pay for a date.

Still later his life is further complicated by his love for Maggie (Magdalena) Hinojosa. This is yet an even more profound mistake inasmuch as Maggie is the daughter of Efrain Hinojosa, who is Jesus' superior at the mobile home factory and already regards Jesus as a wetback with poor possibilities of ever earning much of a living. Consequently, Hinojosa threatens trouble if Jesus persists in seeking a relationship with Maggie.

True to form, Jesus does persist. Then, to earn more money in order to wed Maggie, he gets involved in the drug trade. Soon arrested and deported, he nonetheless manages to make his way back only to learn that the car he has been paying on has been repossessed; a $3,000 stash he had hidden in his rented room has been stolen; Maggie is pregnant by him; and Miguel, whom he at last has found, is mortally ill with a blood clot on the brain and a soaring hospital bill.

In Jesus' case, tragedy begets more tragedy. Next, Jesus finds out that it is the scurrilous Ernesto who has stolen Jesus' $3,000 stash from his drug-trade earnings. Moreover, it is also Ernesto who alerted the authorities to stage the raid on illegal workers in which Jesus was arrested and deported. It is all something Ernesto has done before in his career as a professional stool pigeon. Jesus knows—he has overheard one of Ernesto's telephone conversations. Inevitably there is a confrontation, then a fight. In the course of their struggle Ernesto produces a gun, but then loses the weapon to Jesus, who fatally shoots the accused thief and traitorous informant.

Jesus is swiftly arrested, charged with Ernesto's murder. In addition, Jesus also has been fingered as a drug supplier. Though things certainly look bleak, a visit from Maggie raises Jesus' spirits. Lawyers are expensive, but perhaps Maggie can raise enough funds to mount a legal defense.

In the end there will be no need for her even to try. Within the sordid confines of his shared jail cell, Jesus is about to be initiated into one of the prison rituals. His three black cellmates attempt to rape him. Infamy is added to the disgrace of incarceration. In the ensuing fight, Jesus is fatally stabbed.

If Jesus is thus free of further pain and suffering, one can only assume that those left behind are not. The pregnant Maggie, the stricken brother Miguel, the poverty-stricken Camacho family back home in the nameless Durango village who had depended on the two brothers to make good in the land of the gringos—there, too, one can only assume that they will prevail. The novel is silent on such issues.

Son of Durango is an intensely graphic but flawed work that might well be subtitled *The Brief and Bitter Life of a Modern Wetback.* Indeed, Jesus Camacho seems a composite, the tragic if somewhat stereotyped image of the illegal immigrant macho and the waiting string of disasters ready to befall him on the far side of the magic curtain through which he has passed. The traditional illegal border crossings continue—more rampant than ever, in fact. But times have changed; new technologies—some of them almost incomprehensible—have dramatically altered the job field, the labor force itself, and reinvented styles of life have created an even more alien world. This is borne out by both the setting and the problems encountered by illegals working in a highly complex urban area. Priddy, a Fort Worth attorney, well understands the attendant difficulties of undocumented workers coping in the unnerving sprawl of the combined Fort Worth/Dallas area known as the Metroplex.

The end goal is money, as it always has been. But the United States is no longer an agricultural country seeking pastoral peasants for the stoop labor of harvesting and crop work in the fields at low pay. Jesus and Miguel are exemplary. Both put in short stays at the modest Tackett ranch, soon disappearing into large metropolitan areas where there are not only more lucrative jobs but anonymity and a greater network of Spanish-speaking enclaves into which they can blend and escape little notice.

There is also far greater mobility, but not without its price. In the mobile culture of the automobile, cars not only are status symbols, they are necessities as well. Equally they are entrapments in particular for those with little or no job security and working at the low end of the pay scale. Repossesions are commonplace and, for used car dealers with few scruples, very profitable—here are products that can be sold and resold, time and time again.

Still, though, even an outlandishly overpriced conveyance can be used to turn a profit for the purchaser willing to assume further risk in contraband activities within an alien culture wherein the use of illegal drugs flourishes to the point that, even for petty dealers in the drug traffic, small fortunes can be made. And therein, too, Jesus Camacho fills the bill of typical stereotyping in the increasingly less humane world of the twenty-first century. If Jesus is a victim of his own passions, his shortcomings, even his heritage, along with sundry self-fulfilling prophecies, he is also the victim of a culture that, perhaps in response to an already vastly overpopulated world, uses up people in the lower rungs and casts them out as but so many discards. It is a culture that the Camacho brothers could never have imagined. Their lamentable fate is all the more tragic in its consequence.

12

Before the Gringos Came and After: The Romantic Heritage

An outstanding attempt to document a part of the cultural change that regularly sweeps across the magic curtain is the vintage work of Walter Nordoff, *The Journey of the Flame.* A one-book author, Nordoff, writing under the pseudonym of Antonio de Fierro Blanco, constructed what is essentially but a single year in the boyhood of long-lived Juan Obrigón, the son of an Irish seaman and a native woman of the village of San José del Arroyo in the starkly beautiful peninsula of Baja California.

The Irish mariner, having jumped ship, settles among the inhabitants of San José, but then, heeding the call of the sea again, after about one year he departs. Like Claud Garner's *Wetback* hero Dionisio Jesús Molina, young Juan Obrigón, the child resulting from the union, is left with little more legacy from his father than his red hair, for which he becomes known as Juan Colorado, or "The Flame," and the surname of O'Brien, which soon is Hispanicized into Obrigón.

Once more, the classic hybrid, and the father who never returns. Despite early hardships young Juan not only attains manhood but as well an exceptional lifespan, reaching from his birth in 1798 to his death in 1902. This gives The Flame the perspective for viewing three centuries of change in the cultures of what once were the Three Californias: northern Alta or Upper California which eventually would become a part of the United States, and the two divisions that were to comprise the northern and southern sections of the thousand-mile-long peninsula known as Baja or Lower California.

The Journey of the Flame, in essence, recounts a monumental journey, the 1,500-mile trip of young Juan as a member of a redoutable group in the service of Firmin Sanhudo, inspector-general for the Spanish Crown in the Three Californias. The formidable excursion and expansive survey of the Spanish lands thus extends from the very tip of the peninsula all the way to the singular outpost of Monterey, from which the Sanhudo entourage itself, mission accomplished, sailed for Spain.

Through extensive biographical revelations into the life of The Flame himself, the novel extends far beyond the scope of that single but most significant year of the youthful Obrigón. It is, then, the recollection of that most important episode in the long life of an unlettered but extremely forceful personality. Relating his grand adventure on his hundredth birthday, The Flame is still absorbed in his personal quest, his unfailing attempt to wring some meaning from it all, amidst the imponderable transformations that have enveloped his century of living. Nordoff brings to life the force of change with his portrayal of that long-ago episode that speaks for itself of the way things once were in the Spanish Californias before they became a part of the Republic of Mexico, and still later, before the gringos came, and Alta California was absorbed by the youthful America.

Juan Obrigón's story of his singular journey then is not only a partial chronicle of nineteenth-century life in the storied Californias but as well a miniature portrait of that other California which was cut adrift with the creation of the international boundary in 1848 and the subsequent passing into

American hands of the northernmost part of the olden Spanish California. The Flame has seen, been witness to, it all and has passed across both sides of the magic curtain.

Childless Juan Colorado, the narrator who "died alone" after more than a century of life in 1902, voices its passing in a final statement: "Now all is gone. These southern California Missions, built of adobe, when once unroofed melt away in the rains as quickly as Christianized Indians also disappear. . . ."

Thus in emphasizing the faded past there is less need to contrast the vital present. Here and there, however, The Flame, a sort of oral genius, departs from his account in order to inject some pithy statement to which he clings as one man's truth. "It is a great help to be distrustful," advises the centenarian hybrid hero, "for distrust is the parent of long life."

Certainly that partitioner of the magic curtain through whose veins the blood of both cultures flows seems qualified to speak on that aspect. Even so, Juan Colorado's thoughtful asides and reflections are commonly the views absorbed from his rural background and the simple but so very functional teachings of peasant life. The guitar, for example, that most ubiquitous musical instrument of Latin culture and gentility, says The Flame, "has its uses in life as well as its pleasures, for it teaches the inutility of discords."

But it is with such musings and brief departures from the narrative that Nordoff, alias Antonio de Fierro Blanco, whose sobriquet seems to add the touch of Hispanicized authenticity to the chronicle, is able to call attention to both the lost culture and the faded if romanticized grandeur that once was the whole of the Californias, and the magic curtain was raised for glimpses on both sides. Spanish, and subsequently Mexican, California would live on only in some of the stories of Bret Harte or the Hollywood exploits of the legendary Zorro, much as O. Henry and later the southern California filmdom also rang up the magic curtain to reveal the richly embroidered domain of the Cisco Kid.

❦ ❦ ❦

Aspects of the same Hispanic heritage have been set afoot farther east by the New Mexico novelist Harvey Fergusson in *The Conquest of Don Pedro.* Although the title sounds as if it were a person, Don Pedro is instead an upriver Rio Grande village, and the protagonist an itinerant peddler, Leon Mendes, who settles there shortly after the American Civil War.

Unlike Nordoff's epic peregrination of The Flame, that is largely confined to the vast area of Baja California that belongs to Mexico, Fergusson's story is concerned with what has remained a stronghold of Spanish America rather than Mexican America and the exceedingly close-knit society it long entailed. Don Pedro, though, is almost a border town itself, "nearly as old as El Paso, less than a day's ride to the south."

Nor had the peddler Mendes simply gone there all at once. A native New Yorker and a Jew of Portuguese extraction, he had taken up the trade of roving merchant with the hope of curing his tuberculosis by dint of hard work and exercise in the arid climate of New Mexico. Thus at the age of twenty-eight he had quit New York "with a weak lung, a bad cough and three hundred dollars in cash." In short, Mendes is prepared to cross the magic curtain; his very life depends on it. Only after several years on the road in what now is northern New Mexico, however, had he accumulated enough capital to settle down. He would set himself up in a mercantile enterprise of some permanence, a store, and in a more agreeable climate than that of the hard winters of the Sangre de Cristo Mountain ranges, the village of Don Pedro a little farther south.

Meanwhile, of course, the astute Mendes has undergone the appropriate transformation, the necessary rebirth proscribed by passing beyond the magic curtain. Not only has he acquired a mastery of the Castilian tongue but even the customs of the Spanish Americans among whom he had moved daily with all of his wares for so many years, with the exception, it almost goes without saying, of the trappings of Roman Catholicism, ever faithful to his Jewish heritage.

There was something else, too, which had set him apart, helped him to frame his decision to settle farther south: the snobbishness of the wealthy, the *ricos* of the northern valley. Throughout all those years of his perpetual peddling on the road, they had ignored him, his very existence. "As a peddler he had never been able to get past their heavy front doors to sell them so much as a needle," says the omniscient narrator. And while Mendes was not an aggressive man, there was nonetheless "something inside him that wanted to challenge these lords of the earth."

It was a contest not easily won, nor quickly, either. For years the roving dreamer was to remain an outsider—a gringo, of course, but also a Jew, neither of which was socially acceptable in the closed Hispanic community dominated by the proud and aristocratic landowners. Only as his well-stocked store gained renown—and only very slowly at that—did his status rise.

Mendes prospers, becomes, with reservations perhaps, an acceptable figure and even the paramour of the wife of Agustín Vierra, the most powerful landlord in the community. Yet always the storekeeper remains a figure quite apart. Penetration of the magic curtain never, of course, implies equality in social standing. Not until Mendes finally marries the niece of Vierra does he achieve something of a place for himself within the highly structured and carefully graded society of Don Pedro.

Mendes had liked the girl Magdalena even as a child and she had returned his affection, wedding him at the age of sixteen. She had done so despite the social ostracism the non-Catholic alliance created, ironically, following her return from schooling in Santa Fe whither she had been sent to attain the necessary decorum and pedigree in the social graces deemed necessary for attracting a suitable mate in the higher echelons of the community strata. But only time itself, coupled with the sound financial assistance that Mendes is able to render the monetarily strapped Vierras, helps overcome the deep wound in the social system the newlyweds have gashed open by their unorthodox alliance. Yet through it, the gringo-Jew-ex-peddler has at last arrived, having become now "fully a Mexican gentlemen and the head of a Mexican family."

Still, in passing through the magic curtain it is not enough. After all, it is but the veneer of the other culture, the imagery, which the prosperous merchant has acquired. Not only his heritage but his middle-class background are both against him. The nouveau riche, the upstart, the intruding latecomer never can be one of them. Soon he is to lose even the affections—never too sound to begin with—of his young wife. She will succumb to the charms of a Texan who has more suitable credentials, including youth; indeed, the Texan will become the only other "American" ever to have lived within the all but closed world of Don Pedro.

In a selfless and sacrificial gesture, Mendes quits the town, leaving his bride free to marry his rival. The stage is set for the transitional rise of the magic curtain and Anglo domination. Mendes himself decamps for the northern border country where the transcontinental railroad already is pushing the frontier into the "slow-moving, soft-spoken life that lived in the quiet adobe towns, in the old recumbent houses, the life of the long siesta and the leisurely meal, a life with gaiety and passion about it but no hurry at all and little violence."

It is that hinterland of old New Spain to which Mendes the outsider returns. Too long, Fergusson implies, Mendes had dwelt in that older world that soon is destined to be destroyed. For a while the wandering Jew had found peace, at least of a sort, in a Catholic community no less and even a home, or the superficial trappings of one. But the Portuguese Jew was not ever sufficiently equipped to span the two worlds which were being forged along the incipient border that would contain the magic curtain, an Anglo Protestant one and the Hispanic Catholic entity.

He could resent the newer order from which temporarily he had escaped, but his early years had tied him too much to it; and with the disintegration of his shaky marriage his lack of roots and only superficial cultural ties with that alien and near-border community of Don Pedro had died. Indeed, it is doubtful that they had ever lived. Mendes had crossed the magic curtain but only, particularly as a Jew, to confront the frontier of his own being, his heritage, social standing, career, in short, his very self.

Now he must cross back to the other side of that mirror that forces one to look within oneself at the frontier of the mind, the head, the heart, the spirit of what one is. He will come back, emerge on the other side of the looking glass formed by the magic curtain. Retreat was really all that remained open to him. To have lingered, much less to have set out for areas farther southward, would but have contributed all the more to that alienation that he had challenged but never conquered in a broad and alien land.

It is more than symbolic that Mendes is both Jew and Portuguese and his penetration of the magic curtain is encumbered by those trappings, and that he will emerge on that farther frontier of the ancient Spanish borderlands that once reached much farther north. There is a moment when each must acknowledge it is time to leave; only for a few is the magic curtain that of the final escape.

❦ ❦ ❦

Highly exemplary of that approach is the collection of stories by James Cabell Brown, a truly vintage work of the nineteenth century entitled *Calabazas; or Amusing Recollections of an Arizona "City."* Brown, like Nordoff, a one-book author, and like Lea, illustrator of his own work, wrote in a style that Damon Runyon might well have studied and of a setting reminiscent of the tales of Bret Harte.

Brown's task is to describe the birth, death and something of the social history of the short-lived town of Calabazas (Gourds) set down in southern Arizona. Since the bulk of Calabazan history is neither long nor impressive, a single chapter suffices for that, leaving six tales that recount the lives—or, at any rate, the Calabazan tenures of residence—of its more famous if less illustrious citizenry.

Inevitably, as Brown notes, there was the Calabazas Kid, the young badman whose sobriquet was one designed to express not only his callow youthfulness but also the locale by which his fame had sprung. Inevitably, too, there is the Calabazas Widow and the Calabazas Baby, since these unfortunates have been with us in all times and places and certainly no less in even so pioneer a setting as the dubious outpost of civilization known as Calabazas. Much the same might be said for the itinerant preacher, justice of the peace and, of course, the town club, the latter serving chiefly as sponsor for local games and sundry contests of physical prowess on which friendly wagers could be laid.

The town itself had been founded on property belonging to one of those hallmark companies of the frontier West that speculated in real estate, cattle and minerals. In this case, only two of those windfalls predominated, and so the town was itself "a newly born child" of the Calabazas Land and Mining Company, which, Brown informs his readers, "claimed all the earth from the Mexican boundary to as far north, east, and west as they conveniently or safely could." It was thus not so much what Calabazas actually was which counted but rather what most if indeed not all of its citizens were convinced that it could become. Its path to greatness, then, they believed, lay in the genteel American belief in progress toward vast riches born of real estate and doubtlessly the fruits of the earth it concealed. In Calabazas, as elsewhere, that would be brought to fruition in the usual frontier manner of genial fraud and vacuous speculation.

Much of such optimistic chicanery was already sufficiently in hand, to the point that the Calabazas citizenry even then was engaged in the spirited ritual of community rivalry. Notwithstanding the absence of a promotional chamber of commerce, the internationally situated community had embarked on a sustained feud with its neighbor, the town of Tubac, and had contrived to elicit other rivals. However, the Calabazans had failed dismally in seeking to extend their zesty sense of competitive progress in trade and commerce to the boundary town of Nogales, which housed a "highly esteemed mescal distillery, and the Mexican Custom House buildings." Rivalry there, of course, would have been unwise if not suicidal inasmuch as Calabazas had its own unofficial customs agency in the personage of John Drinkwater and the several merchant pillars of the community who themselves retailed the famous Nogales spirits over the bars of their own saloons.

It was the liquor dealers alone who fostered what air of stability there was in Calabazas. And, correspondingly, through their material success, it was they alone who were able to maintain such standards of conduct and sumptuous styles of life as were deemed good and worthy of emulation.

Yet all of that, what might be seen as essentially a substantial part of the shaping of the American character in the frontier West, is largely extraneous to Calabazas and its vital link with the magic curtain of the international boundary—"the Line," to Calabazas denizens. What is so highly significant in this primal contribution to border literature is that each of the stories culminates with the departure of the protagonists either to or across the Line.

The border itself is the magnetic attraction. For the people of Calabazas the magic curtain extracts, like obituary notices, habitually from the populace, and with the timely thoroughness of inescapable destiny. Even though there are other neighboring hamlets, villages, towns and communities to which the

Calabazans might be drawn, those are notoriously lost sight of in the overpowering presence of the magic curtain, the Line, and the exotic, the enchanting allure it constantly exerts upon them. One by one, the less substantial members of Calabazas are seduced by the border.

Finally, following an outbreak in the practiced ritual of exerting mob violence on neighbor Chinese immigrants who had, in Calabazas as in so many other outpost areas on the western frontier, attempted to take up residence there in peace and goodwill, even the more settled inhabitants of Calabazas make ready to light out for the magic curtain. There is, after all, now little left to induce them to remain in the town. Eventually, even the town's celebrated gentry, composed of such colorfully eminent personages as Bottle Bob, Casino Harry and Handsome George, are themselves forced to call it quits and join the migration into Mexico.

As Brown puts it, those "prominent citizens could no longer stand the peacefulness of the town." Oblivion was already at the threshold of the local watering holes. "The Pantheon, Coliseum, Golden Fleece, and Big Casino were rolled up and piled on wagons, with their chairs, tables, gambling paraphernalia, and bars, and the procession solemnly wended its way to Nogales, that dragon on the Line, that had swallowed up their friends and patrons, who now, in moments of safety, can step over the Line, and free from care or anxiety, shuffle the nimble poker chip, or add a notch to their pistol hilt, and more blood to their record."

In the annals of border literature, Calabazas is unique in its nearly wholesale migration of populace across the magic curtain. The contract of the two cultures is obvious if restrained. Life on the other side always is whatever it is not on the opposite side. If the one is eternal, then the other is ephemeral. If the other appears chaotic, then the one seems possessed of a certain order and stability. If the one is too earthy, the other can make room, and does, for the vast failures and foibles that are an inherent part of the human condition. What one can absolve, the other, failing that, at least can live with.

Calabazas itself, built but a few miles from the international line, eventually succumbs to it, and thus is swallowed up by one of the principal border towns to which it had served a cursory apprenticeship. In it lies a lesson: Not only could the genuinely Anglo settlement not stand in its pure and transplanted state, it created such a vacuum that it caved in upon itself. It is not strange that the border itself should dominate all else in the end. The magic curtain alone serves to emphasize the importance of that transitional zone, the enchanted curtain through which one passes, after which one is never quite the same again.

13

The Quest for Psychological Reality

As the international boundary becomes a settled fact, an institution, penetration of the magic curtain becomes attuned to the psychological realities of the protagonists of border literature. Crossing the border is a physical reality, a concrete fact; reconciling that action with what ensues is quite another. The two cultures separated by the magic curtain are more than merely distinct; in many ways they are opposing forces, opposites of one another, the mirror image that is the other side of what the looking glass reflects. It is as if the ancient saying might be paraphrased: Mirror, mirror on the border, who's the sorted, who the sorter?

The novels that take in hand that concept are, except for a couple, set in the rugged fastness of northwestern Mexico and never far below the international boundary; thus the fluttering of the magic curtain is always offstage, the vast desert and semidesert countryside an impartial audience to the events. Two are vitally concerned with the border as a cultural as well as a political line of demarcation. In Glendon Swarthout's *They Came to Cordura,* the protagonists are in Mexico's immense northwestern territory because of the international incident caused by Pancho Villa's alleged crossing of the border and subsequent attack on the near-border town of Columbus, New Mexico. In Carlos Fuentes' *The Old Gringo,* the imaginary conclusion of what ultimately befell the journalist and short-story writer Ambrose Bierce when he disappeared in Mexico in 1914 during the chaotic years of the Revolution, the psychological realism of penetrating the magic curtain is carried to its apex.

Only in B. Traven's ironic novel *The Treasure of the Sierra Madre,* is modern psychological realism traded for an allegory of the timeless dimension, the quest for happiness via the pursuit of riches. As much fable as adventure yarn, the novel is representative of the endless attempts of outsiders penetrating the magic curtain with the aim of exploiting the legendary mineral wealth in that stark land of sierras and barrancas. While all three novels are descriptive excursions of North Americans in the country south of the border, only in Traven's tale are two of the three central characters won over, claimed, and ultimately adopted by the land and its people whom they would exploit, notwithstanding the fact that their ensuing Mexicanization is less through their own efforts than through the force of circumstance.

The Treasure of the Sierra Madre is dutifully concerned with Mexican life as it stumbles into contact with some outside force, particularly erstwhile representatives of some greater technological and materialistic order, essentially the United States, and in parallel form, Mexicans themselves as agents of bureaucracy and materialism. Generally speaking, the themes are built along the lines of corporate as well as individualistic imperialism. And the protagonists, whether foreign expatriates or merely regional aliens in the heterogeneous complex of cultures of the Republic of Mexico, thus always work at cross purposes with a rustic populace whose habits of thought and outlook are quite at the other end of a gap that, like the magic curtain itself, can be passed though but never fully parted.

Much of that friction is in the underpinning of *The Treasure of the Sierra Madre,* not only in both the 1934 and 1935 English versions of the work but in the film itself, which, far more than most cinematic portrayals of novels, closely adheres to the original work; so that, in effect, three versions of the tale are around, though with only minor variations. In sum, two Americans who have been drawn to Mexico during the boom years of oil exploitation by foreign corporations during the early 1900s eventually run the cycle of rags to riches only to find themselves without the means later to maintain what they have come to consider their proper standard of living.

In a chance meeting with an aging prospector who has served a long apprenticeship in possibly most of the gold fields of the Western world, the two are persuaded to join the old man, half philosopher, half fool, in an effort to extract the precious metal from a site in the border state of Sonora, a site of which the old prospector alone has knowledge. In so dramatic a setting and in pursuit of such a golden hoard lies the bulk of the tale, on one level a western adventure story, on another the false quest that is, in effect, the ongoing search for the self.

While the three men succeed in wresting a fortune from the storied mountain chain, a source of mythical riches since the time of the coming of the Spaniards, it is not destined that they shall either keep or enjoy the fruits of their gains. The real treasure, as the novel suggests, is not at all what they seek. Like the magic curtain itself, the quest is filled with pitfalls, the end of it all only a cul-de-sac. The ensuing loss of a fortune in gold by Dobbs, the central figure, and ultimately his own life are significant from the standpoint of true border literature in that it is Dobbs alone who has entertained the notion of smuggling the gold across the border in order to enjoy the newfound wealth in his own culture, his flight back through the magic curtain.

Dobbs, half crazed by the lust for gold, then driven to further irrationality over the prospect of trying to hang onto it, is caught in the folds of the magic curtain. He is trapped. Unable to pass back through it, neither can he remain, not even with his newly exposed and curtained self, which is, alas, the curtain of madness. It might as easily have become a scheme with the other seekers, Dobbs' sidekick Curtin and the grizzled prospector Howard, had they been both less irrational and less schizophrenic than Dobbs. Indeed, the point can be made that it is an underlying comment on the two cultures beyond the magic curtain that it is Dobbs who opts for a return to the United States, a culture that is more nearly befitting of his confused and psychotic state.

Certainly even Dobbs in his more rational moments can grasp the logic in taking the booty to some interior locale where it might be disposed of gradually and in exchange for ready capital rather than risk the hazards of making a run for the border with a pack train of burros carrying the loot. The countryside itself is trackless, in many instances a desert waste. There are the obvious dangers of bandits—perhaps worse yet, of border officials. Rations are short, water is more so. The flutterings of the magic curtain are magnetic, enchanting.

Despite revelatory fleeting moments of rationality, Dobbs can never rid himself of his grand plan to effect a border crossing, virtually yoked to the burros—a prisoner of his loot. Like so many others who have too deeply penetrated the magic curtain, Dobbs, too, would die believing he could pass back through it, even with his illicit wealth—wealth he would have to enjoy once back in the land where lack of riches had made him an inferior. It is a foolish dream, but one in keeping with the materialism of the culture that he feels has shunned him, and so his ultimate dream is vividly kept before him right up to his death at the hands of Mexican bandits and, ironically, the loss of the hard-won treasure, discarded by the robbers who fail to recognize its value.

Once again, the magic curtain giveth, and the magic curtain taketh away. It is rather the two other men, Howard and Curtin, who have had in mind all along to remain in Mexico, even to undertake some sort of business venture there. Which they ultimately do, even though it is to be of quite a different sort from what they might have envisioned had it not been for Dobbs' treachery in aggrandizing the treasure for himself. Graciously, even cheerfully, the two can accept the measureless enchantment unfolded by their acceptance of the magic curtain.

Having lost the objective of their quest, the perspicacious Howard has found for himself yet another calling, again by ironic happenstance, as a healer or medicine man, a *curandero* of far-reaching powers. And so, in one of the villages not far removed from the site of the short-lived success of their mining venture, Howard settles down in rustic contentment. He will obviously profit from the cultural inequity itself: Superstition and superficial knowledge are conjoined; and Curtin himself, it seems understood, will join him as something of a junior partner and disciple in so respected and frequently profitable a calling.

The magic curtain has been rent, the thin seam through which they passed stitched together anew. In the end it is mother Mexico and the land that triumph: the treasure lost, returned to the earth itself, the visionary quest encountered, idled, ground under foot, resurrected into its original self. In border literature, *The Treasure of the Sierra Madre,* in which the often-desecrated land is either side of the magic curtain, reclaims its own, wins out over those who have tried to exploit it. Only the land is eternal, only the magic curtain flutters open, affording an enchanted gap through which to pass.

Virtually overshadowing the book is the film classic itself of *The Treasure of the Sierra Madre,* not only for its close adherence to the novel but for its celebrated cast and authenticity in locale. The entire movie, in fact, was shot in Mexico, both on location in Tampico where the film opens at a decidedly hot and seedy bar in the 1920s or perhaps, at most, the early 1930s, and later near the village of San José Purua, some eighty miles west of Mexico City.

Certainly the feel of both place and clime is authentic; like some half of the Traven oeuvre the novel deals with Americans in Mexico—Americans not gone native but rather very much aware of their American identity, their apartness, particularly Humphrey Bogart as the central figure of Dobbs, who, in something of a W.C. Fieldsian manner, seems a believer in a character's name shedding light on the person. Dobbs, of course, is Fred C. Dobbs, not Frederick C. Dobbs, nor simply Fred Dobbs, but Fred C. Dobbs. Indeed, in Bogart's hands, Dobbs is practically incapable of conceiving himself as a whole entity without referring to himself as Fred C. Dobbs. It's as if the disintegration of the personality, which seems more attenuated in the film than in the novel, were centered on the wholeness of that appellation itself. Indeed, it overrides the significant contributions of bearded Walter Huston as the prospector-philosopher Howard and Tim Holt as a naive and goodly Billy Budd-like Curtin, even that of Alfonso Bedoya as the bandit Gold Hat who confuses the treasure for the trappings in which it is housed.

But the 1948 movie seems assured of its classic place in filmdom as a Warner Brothers triumph, an intense 126 minutes of adventure directed by Walter Huston's son, John Huston, who also wrote the screenplay. Even further authenticity seems apparent, in following the novel, in that a representative of the official B. Traven, using the name Hal Croves, reportedly visited the set many times; Traven, or his literary embodiment, being one of the few who have penetrated the magic curtain, never to reemerge.

❦ ❦ ❦

The story line in Swarthout's *They Came to Cordura* is psychological realism of quite a different order. The tale derives by way of historical fiction from the time of border imperialism on the part of the United States during the years of the Mexican Revolution. In what turned out to be a burlesque pursuit of

Pancho Villa and his forces by the Punitive Expedition of General John J. Pershing during 1916-17, the United States cavalry engaged in several skirmishes with north Mexican revolutionaries in Chihuahua, the republic's largest state and a principal battlefield of the celebrated cause.

In an effort to catch and punish Villa for his alleged role in the infamous raid on the small town of Columbus, New Mexico, and further anxious to preclude any such additional spilling over of revolutionary activity on American soil, the United States deployed an expeditionary force that, from the outset, was unable to cope with the Villistas on their own terms. Essentially, it was the old story of a better-equipped army being weighed down by its technologically superior ordinance and outmaneuvered by a lighter force of guerrillas fighting on their home ground. Mismatched from the beginning, the American force was a poor combatant for the Centaur of the North and his dedicated followers. Everything was against the Americans, from public sentiment to poor supply lines and heavy artillery that was virtually useless in a guerrilla type of campaign; even the American soldiers' clothing was a handicap in the hot desert clime.

Much has been made of those times in an effort to rationalize and explain so poor a showing on the part of a superior American force. Decidedly those were the waning years of a declining United States Army cavalry, but, technologically speaking, the cavalry was far from being at death's door as a fighting enterprise.

Even so, the Punitive Expedition acquitted itself none too well at such battlegrounds as Aguas Calientes, Carrizal, Guerrero, Temochic—even at Parral, Villa's adopted hometown, where he was assassinated years later. Ultimately, at a place known as Ojos Azules in the south of Chihuahua and just to the north of the Sierra Tarahumara—perhaps symbolic the name, Blue Eyes, for the fair-skinned and often blue-eyed American soldiery—one of the squadrons under Pershing's command led the final charge in that tormented campaign. *They Came to Cordura,* then, is an imaginary tale concerned with "certain minor fictitious events before and after the lost, last charge at Ojos Azules."

A short novel of rapidly paced action, the tale focuses on a series of incidents that befall a small detachment of United States soldiers and a lone American woman in their flight to a point of safety beyond the scope of fighting in northern Mexico. The troops, having been cited for bravery in action, are each to be awarded the Medal of Honor. It has fallen to a major named Thorn (the name perhaps again symbolic of the thorny cactus vegetation of the land) to make sure that the men at least live long enough to be presented their esteemed decorations.

For personal reasons not immediately apparent to Major Thorn, however, each of the men is genuinely disturbed at having been singled out for what for each of them is a dubious distinction. To themselves, their own acts of heroism are suspect; moreover, Thorn himself has broken under fire. Removed as executive officer, Thorn has been made awards officer for the select five troops. Thus it is the military coward Thorn who finds himself cast in the role of hero maker as well as hero finder since it is he who will write the citations for the men.

In short, the high honor for which the troops have been tagged is a folly of discredit, and Thorn's mission is fraught not only with the mental and emotional pain of self-discovery, but of coming to terms with his as well as the others' own basic character. The facts, of course, eventually will come out; the record is inescapable. Thus, in saving themselves from the enemy without, the select group is but preserving itself for extenuating punishment.

As a result they hang back in their limbo of despair and frustration. There is only the dedicated but naive Thorn to goad them into making their way to an ironic safety. The woman, too, a ranch owner in Mexico and the daughter of a less-than-reputable United States senator, is, like the troops themselves, less a willing member of the squad than, in effect, a military prisoner. Adelaide Geary, a woman "more sinning than sinned against," has become faced with the likely possibility of loss of citizenship for having quartered Villistas on her ranch.

The terrain is formidable, the trek itself an endless journey into the interior debate of heroism versus cowardice, and the stresses of coming to terms with both or either. Thorn is confronted with a hopelessly difficult if perhaps not possible a task; it is fraught with hazards from the outside as well as, closer at hand, from within those under his command. Violence repeatedly erupts, then adulterated lust. Finally mutiny runs its ugly course in the murder of the overly conscientious and fatally introspective major.

While the book itself is better than the slow-paced film of the same name, the focus of both is so centered on the psychological irony of the situation that the overall background that has inspired it is for the most part lost. In the movie, even Gary Cooper in the role of Thorn, along with such seasoned performers as Van Heflin and Tab Hunter cannot make director Robert Rossen's 1959 cinematic production come off as much more than an arduous journey rife with petty personal feelings and conflicts. Nor does Rita Hayworth as the Geary woman emerge as more than a token figure—the lone female among six sex-starved men. Perhaps two hours and six minutes are simply too long for so plodding a story in which the border country becomes less a curtain of escape than a monotonous desert-sea as the backdrop for a seemingly endless trek across a wasteland and a final confrontation for the six survivors with themselves, their shortcomings as well as their basic human qualities.

Like other border literature, *They Came to Cordura* exploits but a small part of the vast region contained by the magic curtain and its exotic heritage. It lays open, quite brutally, some of the character of the harsh country. At the same time it serves to portray a segment of that chaotic interval of border history when Mexicans took destiny into their own hands in a revolt that would change their lives forever after.

As historically derived fiction it is distinctive in capitalizing on the most extensive venture of American soldiery in Mexico. The tale stands out as rather a cosmopolitan foray in the domain of border literature as well as a continuing quest for novelistic themes forged under the background of the magic curtain. But of the seven, only the woman has crossed the magic curtain, more or less of her own free will. The men are not there by choice; indeed, it is as if they had never crossed at all and are little more than a chorus of ghostly presences. Only she will pay the price for having penetrated fully the magic curtain of escape and having succumbed to forces quite beyond her, a victim of countervailing forces in the curtain's mirrored imagery.

❦ ❦ ❦

Apart from its place as a border novel, *They Came to Cordura* is also one of the two novels in border literature to deal seriously with aspects of the United States' embroilment in the Mexican Revolution during the chaotic years of 1910-20. But while Swarthout's work achieves its broader appeal in its dissection of heroism, Carlos Fuentes' *The Old Gringo* has its universality in the direct clash of the two cultures along the magic curtain. Indeed, so much is made of crossing that frontier that it becomes not only synonymous with death and life but also with those interior frontiers of the mind and of the heart.

The magic curtain is the embodiment of it all, a curious weaving of realistic settings and fantastic events hung on a canvas of peculiar chronology and fictionalized historical facts. While at one level *The Old Gringo* may be said to be an intense and rather passionately individual study of the contrasts between Mexico and the United States, at another it is simply another western adventure yarn and a surrealistic romance. At its most basic level, it is really the dichotomy of a ménage à trois stemming from the imaginary fate of Ambrose Bierce, the

American journalist and short-story writer who disappeared in Mexico in 1914.

The choice of Bierce as the central figure is noteworthy. A practitioner of yellow journalism, grand master of literary invective, of the printed barb that can kill, embittered by his personal and family life as well as his career, his endless satires and continuing sense of irony and above all his legendary disappearance, which necessitates a question mark after the assumed year of his death—all of this makes Bierce, the old gringo himself, a prototype of the American in Mexico. And beyond that, he is the penetrator supreme of the magic curtain.

Bierce, as seen through the eyes of the Mexican novelist Fuentes, not only has crossed the frontier and gone to Mexico, he has gone there with one purpose, to die. Mexico has always been good at administering death, especially the ancient Mexicans, the Aztecs. It was and remains very much a special part of the whole culture, the Day of the Dead, or *Día de los muertos,* itself a high holiday. And, during the years of the Revolution, Mexico became singularly adept at death. Villa was, among other things, a grand executioner. So were his followers, particularly his *dorados,* his gilded ones, his "golden boys" as they become in the novel.

The implication is clear: Death is the grand reality, the so personal frontier we all carry within, deep inside ourselves. Especially during the epochal decade from 1910 to 1920 death could come at any moment, and benevolently at the hands of others—sometimes those nearest you, because trust was sacred, suspect treachery was rewarded swiftly with a bullet, no questions asked. And trust itself is evanescent, the shadow of doubt a constant and a commonplace. Villa would be the final authority, the giver of life and death. Revolution is not only patricide but fratricide as well. Thus one of Fuentes' characters can exclaim that they are all Villistas now.

But if the enemy is within as well as without, there is still a further enemy, the unequal and imperial land with which a common border or frontier is shared. And so the token gringo shall remain nameless in the mouths of Fuentes' emissaries of death. The old gringo is the personification of those differences contained within the magic curtain, the frontier not only of cultural distinctiveness but of that final frontier itself, the self, and its ultimate end.

The curtain flutters, the old gringo passes through. He has gone there to meet—to make—his own brand of euthanasia. And, of course, he will be obliged for his efforts. A national drama is being staged on the other side; he had felt the intensity of it when first he crossed the border at El Paso and over into Chihuahua, Pancho Villa territory. Already it was as if he had passed into a different world.

In truth, he has entered another environment altogether. One is changed by passing through the magic curtain; and though Fuentes' views in the novel are more surrealistic than dispassionately objective, there is a contrast drawn of towering distinctions between those lands and peoples which the magic curtain draws together but also continually separates. The one, the United States, is a country so devoted to the idea of progress that it obliterates the past; the other, Mexico, is quite unable to forget its conquest and its uncompensated bloodshed. Thus a land of changing seasons but "without memory" faces a land of eternal summer and "memorious dust."

In *The Old Gringo* it becomes the very present and uneasy tension of unequals. Its stock characters are the activists of their appropriate heritages, fomenting a clashing of the ideals of order and democracy, of individual will as opposed to chaos and collectivism, the mastery of one's own destiny gone quite astray. Even the old gringo will, in a manner of speaking, be killed twice—shot in the back, then resurrected on Villa's order so that he can be properly executed with bullet holes showing in the front of his body. It is, once again, more magic realism, fictionalizing Bierce's death after the fate of William Benton, a Britisher whose connections with the great hacendados marked him as enemy of the Revolution by a Villista who bludgeoned Benton to death. In an attempt to ameliorate the ensuing international scandal, Villa had the body exhumed, properly executed and shipped home.

So, too, will die General Tomás Arroyo, the gringo's executioner, at the hands of Villa himself. Only the American woman, Harriet Winslow, center of the stormy if Freudianesque contest between Arroyo and Bierce, will prevail. Dutiful to the end, her missionary-like zeal intact in her service as English teacher to the charges of the once-powerful Miranda family on its vast ranch, she alone will re-emerge from the magic curtain along with, of course, the body of the old gringo, Harriet's mental and spiritual lover, and now destined to occupy the empty grave of the long disappeared father who abandoned her.

Apart from the place of the novel as an unusual romance of mythic complexity, *The Old Gringo* is an impassioned if highly subjective attempt to unravel at least a part of the psychology underlying Mexican and American relations and that ever-magic curtain popularly known as both border and frontier. Or, as Fuentes has one of his characters say, paraphrasing the old gringo's remarks on the Americans' loss of the frontier, save that to the south of them, the border is really not a border at all, but rather a "scar."

So, too, then is the frontier subsumed into self, that "secret frontier" within each of us, including "our differences with others" as well as our own "battles with ourselves." To Fuentes we are all "the object of another's imagination," and so it is that in crossing that secret frontier and hoping to find only the self there, one finds oneself "more than ever in the company of others."

In short, one has entered that realm of the magic curtain, that enchantment of escape and, as in the case of *The Old Gringo,* that final escape. Myth and reality are one. The curtain has fluttered into momentary transparency, and lo, for an instant we can see the wholeness in what once were two sides.

❦ ❦ ❦

If merely crisscrossing the international boundary is one of the hallmarks of border literature, then *Tom Mix and Pancho Villa* is at the top, no contest. Clifford Irving's epic account of four eventful years during the Mexican Revolution when Mix and Villa rode together, 1913-17, is a galaxy of magic curtain dramas. Indeed, it can barely be contained within Mexico, and the romance, although Irving states he would prefer to call it a "historical fantasy," flutters through the magic curtain time after time, spilling over the border from Texas to Arizona while cutting a great swath through Villa's home territory of the immense state of Chihuahua and all the way to Mexico City.

Mix, the later Hollywood cowboy and eventual circus owner, dashes back and forth across the border so frequently that the magic curtain is virtually suspended while he metamorphoses into a revolutionary, a Mexican (if home is where the heart lies) and finally a man. At the age of twenty-six certainly he has found—and lost—more than most men do in a whole lifetime, including the love of three women, each a statement in ethnic variation and contrast, from the young Jewish Hannah Sommerfeld in El Paso to the Tarahumara Indian girl Rosa Navarro de Guaycavo and the mature German-born Elisa Griensen, the latter with a grown daughter in Berlin and herself a woman able to live on her own in Mexico even in revolutionary days.

While Villa himself is the constellation around which all other characters orbit, Mix is the quintessential border hero with conflicting loyalties, reasonably true to himself and his cause, ultimately a spy, a double agent. In the minds of some, he is a traitor no less for his part in dynamiting an American rail line in an effort to delay United States troops en route to try to catch Villa for his alleged participation in the Mexican sacking of the near-border town of Columbus in New Mexico. Fantasy and fact are stitched together in so fanciful a fashion that even in the topsy-turvy world of revolutionary Mexico the magic curtain itself is virtually frozen in time, a victim of its own enchantment.

And that portion of Villa's relatively short life (1878-1923) so faithfully follows the now-familiar accounts in the crystallization of fact, myth and legend about the great bandit chief and revolutionary, that Villa does emerge larger than life; it is a distillation of the volatile personality born Doroteo Arango and shaped into the character known as Francisco (Pancho) Villa. For many, Villa himself may well be the very essence of the twentieth-century hero in the New World, a combination of Robin Hood, Jesse James, political idealist and social revolutionist all rolled into one, and macho to the core. A womanizer, it is true, but then Villa was a man who loved women—perhaps too much. Nor was he given to the vices of strong drink and tobacco. Sanguinary, of course, but Villa was not really one to sully his own hands with dealing out death to traitors, whether real or imagined; that he would leave to his longtime friend, comrade in arms and apostle of death, Rudolfo ("The Butcher") Fierro, and, in Irving's colorful novel, to Tom Mix, who, in the infamous massacre of more than two hundred prisoners following one great battle, would load the pistols of Fierro who shot them in target practice, one by one.

Whether Mix ever attained the status of being privy to Villa's inner circle of officers and the most private thoughts of their leader as well as a colonelcy in Villa's celebrated Division of the North is as questionable as whether Mix was ever a Villista volunteer in the first place. As a curious if perhaps unanswerable footnote to history it is about as much a burning issue as what ultimately happened to Ambrose Bierce as it is imagined in Fuentes' tale of *The Old Gringo.* Fictionally speaking, it doesn't matter; it is all only so much more theatrics for the magic curtain, but in both works the intensity of the unfolding drama heightens, exacerbated by the momentum of revolutionary activity.

Bierce, paralleling the fate of William Benton as the man who died twice, can become the very essence of gringoism in some of its worst qualities whereas Mix can emerge as the quintessential *norteamericano* champion of liberty, and of the underdog. Both are historical fantasies, just as both are historical romances, too. What is noteworthy is that it took more than half a century for novelists from each side of the magic curtain to tackle the problem, to come to grips with differences on the great stage of cultural as well as political and economic, even of spiritual, divergences.

While books about Villa have become so numerous that it is now virtually impossible to separate the man from the myth, and while certainly a significant number of North Americans fought with him, perhaps the general psychology of the times was long against the United States' fully acknowledging Americans' participation in Mexico's socialist revolution, when, in the early twentieth century, a filtered Marxism was being ushered in along its southern boundary. In the proclamations of Francisco Madero and his ever-faithful disciple Francisco Villa the die had been cast, the Rubicon crossed, the line drawn. Suddenly the magic curtain had lost quite a lot of its patina, its gloss, its shimmer of exoticism in olden quests hopefully affording great profits. A parting of the ways was more obvious than ever.

All revolutions end in betrayal. And, as Irving has Mix suggest, perhaps the Mexican Revolution ended with the death of Villa in 1923. In extracting the high points in Villa's career, Villa emerges as the prototype idealist and defender of the poor and downtrodden, the embodied essence of the gentle Madero's humanitarian goals, few of which would be realized. For a brief while the magic curtain had been raised for its greatest drama in the fight for democracy, for liberty, for the end of dictatorships.

It is significant that both novels take the bloody but bold years between 1910 and 1920 as the backdrop for the raising of the magic curtain in its presentation of focusing on psychological reality in the midst of consternation and chaos and ever-present death. Death, as Fuentes says in *The Old Gringo*, the Mexicans were very good at—it is what has attracted Bierce, like the soaring *zopilotes* of the great Mexican north drawn to carrion. A noble death at least can be something of an atonement, a resurrection, for his long and ignoble service in the opportunistic exploitation and imperialism of such capitalistic magnates as William Randolph Hearst, perhaps of the Protestant ethic itself.

So, too, can Tom Mix—successor to the silent film star William S. Hart, archetypal all-American cowboy and embodiment of democratic freedom—properly answer the call for liberty, join the struggle for the oppressed. Mix is tailored for the role, fluent in Spanish from having grown up in El Paso, and by natural sentiment friend of the revolution, particularly Pancho Villa's revolution. With his knowledge of English and natural-born insights into gringo mentality he can be exceedingly useful to Villa. Once again, the cultural hybrid hero emerges in the wake of his predecessors—Tom Lea's Martin Brady of *The Wonderful Country,* Will Levington Comfort's Bart Leadley of *Somewhere South in Sonora.* But Mix's role is far grander, the drama more socially significant, even inspired. This is revolution, civil strife on a national scale, overthrowing a government the first great objective.

This is not being a hired gun for some powerful and greedy hacendado, not slithering to safety under the magic curtain because there's a posse after you and a price on your head. This is joining an as yet ill-formed and ragtag army because you believe in its cause, its ideals, are indeed willing to die for them. Here is the hybrid hero with noble purpose, a high-level participant in a campaign of widespread purpose, seeking fundamental changes written on a large scale.

It is fashioned out of the reality of that epic struggle, and of Villa—or at least as much of him as is currently acceptable, so interwoven have become the man and the myth. Indeed, the *jefe,* the great chief, necessarily overshadows all else; even the hybrid hero must play second fiddle, token gringo, to the rebel leader, an unlettered peasant genius of sorts risen from peonage and banditry to the threshold of absolute power over the life and death of those within his sphere of influence. Villa, as personification of the other side of the magic curtain and of Mexico, is astonishingly complex merely because he is fundamentally a man of simple tastes, pleasures, aims and ideals. Or perhaps the very complexity is only surface, harbored in the magic curtain itself and in our efforts to see through its many layers of mirrored imagery, Mexicans as well as Americans—North Americans, *norteamericanos* actually, because we are all Americans of this once New World.

Fact becomes woven into fiction, and fiction itself seems to become more vivid than reality. It is an endless and ongoing drama to which the magic curtain plays out its variations on a theme. The surface realities, the differences are always obvious and ever present; it is rather the inner feelings, the interior emotions that are less easily captured. Even though we may know what we are looking at we do not always know what we truly think about it, what we feel about it, or perhaps it cannot all be put into words, even into actions. The imagery itself is suspect, inchoate, the magic curtain itself opaque, always capitalizing on a certain inexactness, as mysterious as a mountain range even after one has crossed it.

Only the land is eternal; in this case the implacable, neutral, timeless desert, as uncaring as the force that gives vitality to the drama unfolded by the magic curtain itself and its mirror image. Here then is really the final frontier, the dissolvement, the dissolution of this chaotically nomadic and senseless whirlwind of movement, indeed, of life itself. For Fuentes, on the one side is a people, who, until the revolution, were unaccustomed to packing up and going anywhere but rather spinning out their lives in the place they were born, and on the other a people beset with unbounded restlessness.

Implacable foes, arch enemies, are the gringo and the Mexican.

Yet through the magic curtain, each, individually, can be reborn into the other. Rebirth into the other world is almost instantaneous on slipping through the magic curtain. In life, as in death, enchantment lies on either side; it is the constant veil through which all pass. Like all else, it is a metaphor, the magic curtain itself the sole reality. What we make of it always is left up to us.

14

The Individual as Outcast in the New Millennium

There is, of course, no final chapter to true border literature. As long as there are tales to be told and stories to be written, the borderlands of novelization will have a place. Yet it is no longer the romanticized and legendary world it once was, and it is all too well known now for innovative authors to take the liberties with the land and the people that they once did.

Some indication, however, of where the literature has been and where it is going can be seen in a quintet of novels: one from the B. Traven oeuvre, four from Cormac McCarthy. The time frames range from the days of filibusters and scalp hunters to the present times of drug traffickers and illegal aliens coping with concrete ribbons of highway, alienating fences and radar-tracking stations. In between is but a single novel indicative of the exploitation of workers in post-revolutionary Mexico. In sum, the novelistic themes are clear: the proletarian worker on foot is a thing of the past; the cowboy is finally unhorsed; the individual survives, but only as an outcast.

Mass culture and high technology herald the arrival of the new millennium. It is McCarthy's border trilogy *(All the Pretty Horses,*

The Crossing, and *Cities of the Plain)* that leads into the twenty-first century. *Cities of the Plain*, the final volume of the trilogy, seems, in fact, light years away from McCarthy's earlier border novel *Blood Meridian, or, The Evening Redness in the West.* Then, pre-revolutionary Mexico was as ripe for group invasion as post-revolutionary Mexico was for individual exploitation, as conveyed in *The Treasure of the Sierra Madre.*

Another novel of B. Traven, *The Cotton-Pickers,* casts a disparate lot of adventurers into the eastern realm of the border country. The locale of the short novel, the state of Tamaulipas and the Tampico area, is purposely vague; the time frame, the early 1920s, a bit hazy. Mexico remains in the midst of pacification after the chaos of the Revolution, but foreign companies still dominate significant sectors of the economy, from oil to banking and from railroads to mining.

Traven's protagonist is Gerard Gales, a character who figures in other novels by Traven as a passive-aggressive individualist who is ever the subversive literary conscience of the underdog. In this instance Gales meets up with five other men, all seeking to hire out to pick cotton on a farm run by an American named Shine. A disparate group, the five job seekers consist of two Mexicans, two blacks, and one Chinese. Gales, the only white man in the group, rounds out the ethnically diverse band whose alleged source of employment is near the village with the unlikely name of Ixtlixochicuauhtepec. Indeed, it turns out that no one has ever heard of any village with so uncommon a name as Ixtlixochicuauhtepec, particularly in that region of northeastern Mexico where, as a conversation establishes early on, much of the land is in the hands of gringos.

Shine is located, however, and the six—Gales and Sam Woe the Chinaman; Antonio and Gonzalo, the two Mexicans; and the two blacks, Abraham and Charley—begin to work for Shine. Traven's abiding concern with the inequities of the social order is soon established by having Shine offer to pay Gales, the lone white man, more than the other workers. Shine, of course, has his own self-interest at heart in pledging such an offer since he believes Gales is an agitator and alludes to "bolshies" (Bolsheviks) in the ranks of the Wobblies, as members of the IWW, the radical Industrial Workers of the World, sometimes were called.

Still more favoritism, and possibly again protective self-interest, occurs when Shine puts Gales in the way of a job at an oil camp where one of the drillers has been injured. That operation, too, is run by Americans; and the job is but temporary. When Gales later returns to put up at Shine's farm, Shine tells him that Charley, the larger of the two black men, left the day after Gales left for the oil camp. And Gales further learns that Gonzalo is dead, accidentally killed by Antonio, whom Gales later encounters in Tampico.

There, too, what work is to be had comes from foreigners. Antonio and Gales both wind up as waiters in a cafe and bakery business run by a French couple named Doux. Thoroughgoing skinflints, the Frenchman and his wife are portrayed as even worse employers than the gringo Americans; so much so that an effort is made to unionize the workers. It is ironically successful—the business is shut down. Although employer and employees come to terms later and the place is reopened, both Gales and Antonio eventually quit, and soon are looking for new jobs.

Once more there are prospective employments, and for Americans as would-be patrons, of course. The job is picking cotton, in an undetermined place called Concordia, for a man designated as G. Mason. Upon arrival, however, a man named Mason informs them he is not the G. Mason mentioned in the note signed by a man named L. Wood, who sent the job seekers there. Rather, he is W. Mason; there is, in fact, no G. Mason at all. Which, of course, is Mason's way of getting out of hiring inasmuch as he has in the meantime been able to hire Indians as cotton pickers and for much less money.

Nearly destitute, Gales returns to Tampico and later lands a job with yet another American, Pratt, who hires Gales to drive a thousand head of cattle some 350 miles overland from Pratt's ranch to an unnamed port, possibly Tampico, on the Gulf of Mexico. At last, in the spate of a series of disastrous jobs, all depicting the exploitation of the working class, the cattle drive for Pratt and Mrs. Pratt, a rough-talking American woman who is attracted to Gales, turns out to be a grand success. Certainly, cowboying wins hands down over stoop labor in the cotton fields.

Cotton, though, remains the central focus of the novel. In fact, serving as a virtual participant in the story is the "Song of the Cotton-Pickers," a sort of IWW-type ballad whose five verses, Gales claims, were taught to the other workers by Gales himself. An adventure yarn of the vagabond life and the nomadic existence occasioned by seasonal work and temporary employment, *The Cotton-Pickers* has many faults, but its criticism of the status quo is not one of them. Racial prejudice, sexual and worker exploitation, xenophobic excess, travesties of law and justice, those are recurrent themes in most of the B. Traven works, from *The Death Ship* to such truly Mexican novels as *Government, The Carreta, The Bridge in the Jungle, The Rebellion of the Hanged, The General from the Jungle,* and *March to the Montería* (originally published as *March to Caobaland*).

Exploitive Americans in the northern borderlands of Mexico is a theme in both *The Cotton-Pickers* and *The Treasure of the Sierra Madre*. Particularly in *The Cotton-Pickers* the intrusion of Americans is so extensive that the locale might as well be southern Texas, as though the significance of the lower Rio Grande as an international border had been swept away. The geographical area is vague, even sketchy. Apart from the attention given to the port city of Tampico, where the Doux couple run their bakery/cafe, and women entertain their male clients in the Golden Quarter, the other locations are nondescript: Shine's farm, Pratt's ranch, the oil camp that is identified only by its number 97, the town of Concordia, the mythic Ixtlixochicuauhtepec village.

In the seemingly authentic and apparently firsthand accounts in the novels of B. Traven, readers of the Traven oeuvre will find ample material for considering those points in Michael L. Baumann's outstanding work in literary sleuthing, *B. Traven: An Introduction.* As Baumann makes clear, possibly several personages were incorporated in publishing the works ascribed to the proletarian writer "B. Traven." One or some of those would have been, as Baumann points out, "only a cowriter, not the original creator of the early Traven works." Possibly, Gerard Gales served as the *Erlebnisträger* ("carrier of the experiences"), Baumann suggests, for the official "B. Traven" works published in Germany.

Baumann, a gifted bilingual scholar, has performed an astonishing job of literary detecting in tracing the publication history of those works, a complicated story in itself. *The Death Ship,* for example, the first novel, was originally published as *Das totenschiff,* in Berlin, in 1926. The second novel, *The Cotton-Pickers,* was published originally as *Der Wobbly,* also in 1926 in Berlin, later renamed *Die Baumwollpflücker* when it was republished in Berlin in 1929. *The Treasure of the Sierra Madre,* the third work, was brought out in 1927 in Berlin as *Der Schatz der Sierra Madre.*

Whatever the corporate literary enterprise "B. Traven" may have been, the books remain the important point. All are, in essence, a framework, a scaffolding on which to hang a tale of adventure in the lives of the exploited, so frequently expressed in the songs and stories of the labor movement as seen through the eyes of Wobblies such as Gales in sympathizing with the IWW movement and commonly depicted as bindlestaff bums and migrant working stiffs. *The Cotton-Pickers* epitomizes such a nomadic existence and capitalizes on exploitation of the lowest rungs of the working class as an international condition that is as bad in the Republic of Mexico as in the United States, and perhaps worse, given the protective status of foreigners with capital and a racist mentality.

On another level, the novel is instrumental in further establishing the great north of Mexico as distinctively apart from the rest of the nation, or, as it often has been said of Mexico itself—so far from God and so close to the United States. As literature of the border country, *The Cotton-Pickers* also rounds out the scope of novelization, from one end of the international boundary to the other, from Tamaulipas/Texas to the two Californias encompassed in *The Journey of the Flame.* A magical world remains on either side of the border; the magic curtain still flutters. There are rents showing in it. but it is still of a piece. The enchantment has not yet eroded into the abrasive hardness and squalid reality of the globalization of mass culture awaiting in the wings, offstage as it were, as an institutionalized and bureaucratized border becomes increasingly used, both legally and illegally, at the turn of the century and the arrival of a new millennium.

❦ ❦ ❦

By far the most ambitious writer in the production of literature of the border country is Cormac McCarthy, creator of a border trilogy published during the years 1993 through 1998, and thus advancing the scope of the work into the new millennium with the final volume, *Cities of the Plain.* The first volume of the trilogy, *All the Pretty Horses,* was brought out in 1993; the second novel, *The Crossing,* was published in 1994. Some groundwork for the trilogy seems to have been laid in 1992 with McCarthy's earlier border novel entitled *Blood Meridian, or, The Evening Redness in the West.*

All the Pretty Horses justly garnered the most acclaim. Romanticized imagery flourishes with boyish heroism, masterful horsemanship, much derring-do, and impassioned young love. It is difficult, in fact, to determine whether McCarthy is writing juvenile literature or adult fiction masquerading as a sort of boys' book penned with mature nostalgia. In any case, it is an engaging blend and a highly readable work by a Tennessean long a resident of El Paso. McCarthy's descriptive powers are brilliantly evocative, so much so that often it seems as if the border country itself is the principal protagonist, as though the harshness of the land had early on well seasoned its youthful characters.

The framework—the canvas, as it were—that the author uses to paint the plot is simple. The youthful protagonist John Grady Cole is seen as a kind of reverse wetback, a *mojado revés*, so to speak. He and a friend, Lacey Rawlins (both are about sixteen years old and have grown up together as pals), set out to ride their horses across the border into Mexico. En route the two are caught up with by an even younger boy, Jimmy Blevins, who is determined to ride with them. Blevins, it turns out, will be the bad actor in the trio and quite soon the cause of their troubles there.

Eventually separated from Blevins, Cole and Rawlins secure jobs in Mexico, unlikely as this might seem, given the long history of Mexico's joblessness. The two sign on as horse breakers for the Hacienda Señora de la Purísima Concepción. It's an 11,000-hectare spread in the border state of Coahuila and is owned by don Hector Rocha y Villareal, whose daughter Alejandra is approximately the same age as Cole.

Not surprisingly, the two become lovers. Equally unsurprising, the ill-starred romance fails to pan out. Nor can the jobs breaking horses endure. Ultimately Cole and Rawlins find themselves unfortunately regrouped with Blevins, who, left to his own miscreant devices, has had his horse stolen, tracked down and shot the responsible culprit and recovered the horse. He succeeds in getting himself as well as his two fellow countrymen jailed as horse thieves. Imprisonment in Mexico is depicted in all its horror. Blevins is killed, dispatched in the age-old fashion: shot while trying to escape. Cole himself narrowly avoids dying in a jailyard fight, ultimately killing a knife-wielding inmate who is trying to kill him.

Winding up the tale, Rawlins returns to Texas. Cole goes back once again to la Purísima and sees his beloved one last time. The hopelessness of any love match is further doomed by a long conversation with Alejandra's sagacious great-aunt. Cole listens far more than he talks, but he is, of course, readily bilingual.

Though romance fails, avenging wrongs blossoms. Somewhat anticlimactically, Cole returns to the town where he had been jailed, takes captive the unprincipled commandant responsible for most of their ills—unjust imprisonment, Blevins' killing, Cole's duel to the death, the seizure of their horses. Death he cannot rectify, but he can get back the horses. Cole is wounded in the course of such action—shot in the thigh—but he manages to get home. En route he stops off to see Rawlins, and then rides on.

❦ ❦ ❦

More mythic boy heroes gallop into action in *The Crossing. Here,* though, the two protagonists are siblings, Billy Parham and his younger brother Boyd. In effect, it would seem to readers of *All the Pretty Horses* that John Grady Cole and Lacey Rawlins have simply resurfaced in a different guise. Once again, horses are at the center of the tale; the Parham brothers are as laconic as Cole and Rawlins and tend to spit a lot; and the story shifts more than once back and forth across the border.

Again, too, the time of these border-crossing adventures is purposefully vague, and McCarthy's descriptive powers abundantly profound. Time and landscape loop in and out like a coiled lariat in the telling of the tale, and horseback is still the means of travel. There is, indeed, a robust amount of riding about from the outset when readers encounter Billy and Boyd living on a ranch with their parents near Cloverdale, New Mexico.

Billy, an environmentalist long before it was ever fashionable to be one, sets out to return a trapped she-wolf to the relatively near mountains of north Mexico. Having accomplished that difficult task he returns home to find his parents killed by Indians, who have also stolen the family horses. Boyd, however, is alive, having escaped such a fate by hiding. Shortly, coming to terms with so horrendous a loss and little heart to remain at the ranch, Billy and Boyd soon cross into Mexico with the goal of recovering the stolen mounts.

Once across the border, more happens to Boyd than to Billy. In the course of numerous adventures Boyd gets badly shot, falls in love with a Mexican girl, and the young lovers get separated from Billy. Eventually Billy loses track of the two altogether and finally rides back across the border, only to discover that the United States is at war. Billy then tries to enlist, but he cannot pass the physical for any of the armed forces. Instead, he spends the next few years as an itinerant cowboy, working here and there for various ranches; never marrying, always moving on, his life a purposeless pursuit of nomadism.

Now, once again, Billy crosses the international boundary, determined to find Boyd, wherever his long-lost brother might be in the north of Mexico. What Billy finally finds, however, is only Boyd's grave. Solemnly he begins to dig up the remains, exhumes the pitiable remnants of what once was his young brother. At least, Billy will bury what's left of his only sibling north of the border, in U.S. soil.

Therein, too, McCarthy's powers of description are unleashed; the author of the border trilogy has a fascination for evil that wells up in depictions of the bleakness of existence, the blackness of the human heart. A section on an old Mexican reliving his personal horror of the Mexican Revolution and how he was blinded by a German mercenary follower of the Huertista faction, who, hugging the Mexican as if to give him an abrazo, instead literally sucked out his eyeballs, easily summons up recoil. A reader is properly repulsed.

As for Boyd, his own tragic but brief life has left at least a thin refrain of memory. Headstrong, determinedly independent, a supporter of the underdog, Boyd, Billy learns, even is celebrated in a corrido. The blond young foreigner is thus elevated to heroic status, reminiscent of the triumphant qualities renowned in the

Ballad of Gregorio Cortez. Like Gregorio, Boyd has attempted to right perceived wrongs, participated in the struggle of *los de abajo*. The fair-skinned alien youth, with gun in hand, was on the side of justice; perhaps he died *con pistola en la mano*. Passage through the magic curtain is fait accompli. The transformation is complete.

McCarthy's preceding study for the trilogy of border country novels also precedes the others in its historical time frame. The title itself, *Blood Meridian, or, The Evening Redness in the West*, is disturbing, subject to misinterpretation, decidedly uninviting. Bloodlust might be a more accurate title inasmuch as the novel is, in essence, one long episode of violence, rooted in historical happenings but forged with excesses of imagined brutality that seem coercive and forced, even incoherent, in its absorption with mayhem and madness. It is a descent into a kind of frontieresque purgatory, even at a time when Anglo filibustering to loot and pillage in Mexico was commonplace, and white renegade scalp hunters plied their ghastly trade.

Here, too, the protagonist is a youth. The kid even is nameless. Readers catch sight of him at age fourteen, joining up with a ragtag group of land pirates bent on plundering Mexico. Still later the kid will sign on with the scalp hunters once the filibustering adventure has disgracefully failed. If the stripling's early initiation into depravity and sordid fiascoes of trying to get something for nothing is not more than individually demoralizing, group degeneracy is mustered from the assemblage with whom the kid has cast his lot.

While those range from the scalp hunter Glanton to a former priest, the derelict cast further includes the ubiquitous gadabout Toadvine, the impious Reverend Green and the villainous Judge Holden, along with racial dichotomy in the guise of a white man and a black man, each named John Jackson. Copious symbolism abounds—later, an idiot, in a cage no less, is picked up; and there is also a dancing bear. If it is an odd lot, it is equally an odd tale, even in the scope of border literature. A final scene is all too telling of the human condition: the setting is a saloon, and the dancing bear is enormously present.

Although rampant greed and an undercurrent of violence well inform *Blood Meridian,* these are not so much manifest as they are apparent sub rosa. And, as in the other two novels in the trilogy, there is really no sex nor sexual violence; there are only allusions to whoring and drunken sprees wherein liquored-up men demand yet more liquor and women as a matter of course. All told, it is a black, bleak, and somber tale of depravity, of lawlessness, and amorality. A damning portrait of humankind emerges.

The hapless kid, ancestral cousin to the luckless Jimmy Blevins of *All the Pretty Horses* and the ill-fated Boyd Parham in *The Crossing,* is thrust into early manhood as the unwitting associate of the villainous *Blood Meridian* crew. Idiocy is caged; the world, as stage, is but a saloon; life is a dance performed by a trained bear and a sold-out judge.

❦ ❦ ❦

Cities of the Plain, Cormac McCarthy's final volume of his border trilogy, furthers—indeed, concludes—the lives of John Grady Cole and Billy Parham. Mature men now, their lives have been profoundly affected by their youthful, individual experiences below the border.

Parham's younger brother Boyd was killed in northern Mexico, whence the two had gone long years ago as mere striplings tracking horse thieves following the slaying of their parents by Indians at the family ranch in New Mexico. Now Cole is destined to forfeit his life in one of the seedier barrios of Ciudad Juárez, El Paso's sister city across the great river.

Having fallen in love with Magdalena, a young Mexican prostitute, Cole has determined to marry her. With Parham's help he will whisk her out of the brothel life into which she has been sold as a young girl from the impoverished southern frontier state of Chiapas and across the border into Texas. Notwithstanding their own straitened circumstances as ranch hands, neither Cole nor Parham would ever consider trying to get something for nothing. Straightforward types out of the mythic Old West, they are fair players in their dealings with everyone; they pay for what they get.

A plan of escape is hatched, to which Magdalena is privy. It is aboveboard. Cole, with much sacrifice on his part, has managed to put together a sum of money with which he proposes to buy Magdalena's freedom. With Parham as go-between, he will strike a bargain with her pimp Eduardo. But no deal is struck. If Parham thinks Cole is crazy, Eduardo knows that he is. Rational men do not fall in love with whores. Obviously, Cole is not rational. In this irrationality there can be no meeting of minds. There can be only trouble. When Cole persists in his plan—his dream—trouble follows immediately. Lured to a false rendezvous, Magdalena soon is found dead in the celebrated river that separates the two lands, her throat slashed.

Cole's late-found reason for living having been taken from him, Cole will avenge her death, confront the suspect killer Eduardo on his own turf, in his brothel den of an office. Eduardo is famed as an exceptional *cuchillero,* but Cole is also a knifefighter of merit. If his skill is less than that of Eduardo, then perhaps his courage is greater.

In the end it does not matter. Both pay with their lives for the very thing that has brought them to such an impasse. Yet the fallen woman, the whore Magdalena (the biblical referent is never opaque), already was no more before they were. Vibrant and Virgin-worshipping Mexico lives so eloquently only because it is a land of death.

It is left to Parham to pick up the pieces, which he does exceedingly well, and in the laconic fashion of those born to the western cattle culture in which there is no room for small talk and few words are wasted. Producing such dialogue is but one of the manifold literary talents of McCarthy, and *Cities of the Plain* is a masterful rendition of such reserve, not only in emotional restraint but in the economy of the telling. There remains only the essence in getting to the heart of the matter.

Inevitably, Parham will quit the ranch where he and Cole have worked together so closely over the years. His loss of Cole as best friend, spiritual brother and kindred soul is irreparable. Each is, in effect, the other's alter ego. Parham cannot bear remaining in a place where so much has been taken from him. He will wander, homeless and alone, ultimately arriving in the new millennium and his seventy-eighth year; a sort of alien exile, afoot and adrift, and taken in by a family residing on the outskirts of Portales, New Mexico. It is all but a vanished life by now. And Parham's declining years may well be taken to be indicative of what is in store for increasing numbers of the human race as a watershed of the past is overwhelmed by the futurism of the omnipotent present and its unbridled technology—on both sides of the border.

Still, there is at least a casual reference to what there is left of life, and it is in Mexico—or at least that part of Mexico has not yet sold out to a Mexican Revolution that once promised so much. But it is that Mexico that had been known to the brothers Parham and to Cole much earlier, in their transition from youth to manhood as captured in the first two volumes of the trilogy, *All the Pretty Horses* and *The Crossing.*

Cities of the Plain does not leave much room for speculation as to where the new millennium is headed. Much of the twenty-first-century setting already is here. Nor is it a particularly triumphant heralding. Witness the aged Parham in the epilogue contending with a fellow vagrant's revelation of a disturbing dream as they shelter themselves beneath a concrete overpass at some nameless spot along the maze of highways in central Arizona—antique travelers in a surreal land. In the distance what appears to be the white dome of some ancient mission church at closer hand is seen to be a radar-tracking station. And moving figures in the night turn out by day to be no more than bits of tattered plastic flapping in the wind against a fence.

Afterword

It would not come again, the fleeting elixir that for a time had cloaked the border country as a mysterious realm. Only the border itself would retain its mantle as the ephemeral curtain through which one transited that realm. A peculiar entity; with time it also lost much of its aura of mystery, the romance that surrounds the little known.

Of the past, not much more than storied images remain. We can barely catch sight of it as it once was. The accouterments of technology engulf us in a standardized urgency. More machines foster yet more technology as more and more people vie for space in a technology-driven world.

At the border itself: more cars, more cargo, more computerization, more border crossings. And with the relentless onset of familiarity, the once-alluring world of the imaginative is swept away. Myth and legend are supplanted by facts and figures. The possible, the prospective—those are no longer there. Reality rushes in. The curtain closes over the drama of the past, and with it, much of the former magic it concealed has vanished.

Possibly we are the poorer for it, for having lost the magical quality that exists in all things and captures our attention, holds it, for so long a time as we are fascinated by our apprehension of its seeming secrets. Indeed, it is the differentness that has attracted us. Only when the extraordinary has become the commonplace is the attraction gone.

When similarity becomes the constant, there is but slight tolerance for variation. The unusual is erased, blotted out. There is little room for uniqueness, for individuality. And the alarming probability of the rise of one world, one mass human culture, one way of doing things becomes all the more apparent. Yet barely has all this occurred before it too has shifted; the utter corporeality has disappeared and even the most recent commonplace suddenly has become the past. The magic curtain through which it has been filtered is once more as transparent as a dream. It had no substance from the outset.

The curtain is but a thing of plain air after all—a conjurer's trick straight out of the trompe-l'oeil school of painting. Only for the moment have we suspended our disbelief. The horses and riders have galloped into history. The ballads are packed away and stored as so much folklore; the novelists now restricted from embellishing as fiction what now is fact. And our world is suddenly much smaller for the loss of it.

Notes on Sources, Readings and Films

That the corrido is still much alive in the United States is perhaps best demonstrated by the numerous ballads evolving from the life and work of Cesar Chavez, founder of the United Farm Workers of America (UFWA) in Fresno, California, in 1962. "There must be more than fifty corridos now about our Movement," Chavez has recalled, "but this was the first one (1962). While we were having our meeting, Rosa Gloria (a worker in the UFWA movement) just started writing. Then, when I got through, she sang it to the tune of 'Corrido de Cananea,' which is about a jail, but which was also the scene of some bitter miner strikes. Her corrido was about our Union, and two of the verses went something like this:

In the year '62
With effort and uncertainty
There began a campaign
For the campesino.

Cesar Chavez started it.
He became a volunteer
And went forth as a pilgrim
To fulfill his destiny.

En el año '62
Con esfuerzo y incierto
Se empezó una campaña
Por el campesino.

Cesar Chavez lo empezó.
Se hizo un voluntario
Y salió como peregrino
Para realizar su destino.

"The theme of the ballad was that I had come, and things were going to be different now. I didn't believe her. But I liked it so much I asked her to sing it at our first Union convention." —J. Levy, *Cesar Chavez: Autobiography of La Causa* (New York: Norton, 1975), p. 170.

The influence of the international boundary itself is so far-reaching in its effects on the balladry of northern Mexico that it is readily apparent in such corridos as that of the bandit hero Heraclío Bernal *(El corrido de Heraclío Bernal)* and *The Beauty of Torreón (La hermosura de Torreón)* as well as the revolutionary ballad entitled *The Sonoran Campaign (La campaña de Sonora)*. It is even more significant in the ballad concerning the persecution of Francisco (Pancho) Villa *(Corrido de la persecución de Villa)* and symbolic in its expression of eminent danger to Mexico when United States troops stood ready to intervene during the Revolution in such a corrido as *El peligro de intervención Americana.*

Correspondingly, a number of border towns and near-border towns and cities figure in revolutionary times as scenes of battles. Fight plans and captures *(tomas)*, such as those corridos celebrating *De la toma de Ciudad Juárez (The Capture of Juárez City)* and that of Torreón *(La toma de Torreón)* or *Del plan de Agua Prieta* and *De la batalla de Naco, Sonora,* etc.

As a point of departure for tracing the heritage of the corrido in the New World, a good starting point is Ramón and Gonzalo Menéndez Pidal, *Romancero* (Madrid: Instituto Escuela, 1936). Particularly insightful, too, are Vicente T. Mendoza's *El romance español del corrido mexicano* (México, D.F.: Imprenta universitaria, 1939); and *Trayectoría del corrido* by Hector Pérez Martínez (México, D.F.: n.p. 1935). Also, *Del Rabel a la Guitarra: El corrido mexicano como un derivado del romance español,* by Margarita Posada Prieto (México, D.F.: n.p., 1944).

Exceedingly helpful as well are Daniel Castañeda's *El corrido mexicano: su técnica literaria y musical* (México, D.F.: Editorial Surco, 1943); *Corridos históricos de la Revolución Mexicana de 1910 a 1930 y otros notables de varias épocas,* edited by Eduardo Guerrero, and also his *La musa popular: Corridos de amor y cantamientos sentimentales del pueblo mexicano,* both works (México, D.F.:, n.p., 1931).

More specialized is *Corridos de la Revolución,* by Celestino Herrera Frimont (Pachuca, Hidalgo: Talleres Linot. del Gobierno, 1934). Sweeping in treatment and broad in coverage are *Hojas sueltas impresas con corridos y canciones,* by Antonio Vanegas Arroyo (México, D.F.: Casa Editora, n.d.); and especially the two-volume work of Higinio Vázquez Santa Ana: *Canciones, cantares y corridos mexicanos* (México, D.F.: Imprenta de León Sánchez, 1942-45).

Like most cultural items taken out of their native element, corridos in translation do not travel well; consequently numerous liberties have been taken in the interpretations, rather than translations of the corridos in *The Magic Curtain,* always with a view to keeping as nearly as possible the spirit and scheme of the rhyme of the ballads, and ever mindful of the ancient maxim of *traditor traditorri.* Grateful acknowledgment is made to those who have passed that way before in the field of the corrido, of border balladry and folklore and its continuing heritage.

Particular tribute is due Brownie McNeil's "Corridos of the Mexican Border" in *Mexican Border Ballads and Other Lore* (Texas Folklore Society, vol. XXI, Austin: Capital Printing Co., 1946, pp. 1-34); to Paul Schuster Taylor's *An American-Mexican Frontier: Nueces County, Texas* (Chapel Hill: University of North Carolina Press, 1934), from which the *Corrido de Robestown* is derived; and to Americo Paredes' *"With His Pistol in His Hand": A Border Ballad and its Hero* (Austin, University of Texas Press, 1958), in which the *Corrido de Gregorio Cortez* achieves a full-scale study.

To see how far the corrido has come in recent times and its celebration of drugs and drug pushers, and the consideration of such ballads by authors dealing with the drug traffic problem, see

Elaine Shannon's *Desperados: Latin Drug Lords, U.S. Lawmen, and the War America Can't Win* (New York: Viking, 1988), especially pages 257 and 345 where Shannon quotes from a ballad celebrating the exploits of the convicted drug trafficker Rafael Caro Quintero and commemorating his capture in 1984. Shannon further quotes from another corrido penned in praise of yet another figure in the contraband drug business, Manuel Salcido Uzeta, otherwise known as Cochi Loco (Crazy Pig) because of his particular viciousness.

More balladry glorifying characters in the contraband drug trade figures in a book by Terrence E. Poppa, *Druglord: the Life and Death of a Mexican Kingpin* (New York: Pharos Books, 1990), which is billed as "A True Story" of the life of Pablo Acosta who was killed in 1987 in the Rio Grande area around Ojinaga, Chihuahua, opposite Presidio, Texas. While one ballad hails Acosta as the "czar of traffickers," yet another exonerates him for simply giving the Americans what they wanted, that is, supplying addicts with the substance needed to support their addiction. Seen in that light, *narcotraficantes* in the era of drug wars are again the underdogs in the ballads of the later conflicts over border contraband. Martyred, as was Acosta in being killed by Mexican *federales,* such drug czars become even more heroic symbols of the underprivileged Mexican caught in the political crossfire of the governments of Mexico and the United States, but particularly the United States viewed in its perennial role as Colossus of the North, arrogant superpower and moralistic guru. In any case, in the era of open drug warfare, the once folkloric and anonymous corrido has moved to higher ground. It's exemplified in the very title of Arturo Carrillo Strong's book, *Corrido de Cocaine: Inside Stories of Hard Drugs, Big Money and Short Lives* (Tucson: Harbinger House, 1990), with its prefatory quote from *The Ballad of Lamberto Quintero* by Antonio Aguilar: "I wish this was only a story, / But, mister, this is the truth."

There are, of course, certain other works that figure somewhere on the outskirts of general border literature but are not actual novels of the border. Another novel by Will Comfort, for example, *Apache* (New York: Dutton, 1931), tells the story of Mangas Coloradas, the outstanding chief of the Mimbreño Apaches, whose eventual cultural breakdown derived from the strife along the Arizona-Sonora section of the international boundary. So, too, does Jane Barry's novel, *A Time in the Sun* (New York: Doubleday, 1962), cover much the same ground, although from a slightly different vantage point. In addition, the anthropologist and novelist Oliver La Farge has depicted much of the life-and-death struggle of yet another Apache leader and his band in *Cochise of Arizona (The Pipe of Peace is Broken)* (New York: Aladdin Books, 1953).

A pair of books by the naturalist-novelist Dane Coolidge cover much the same territory and the lives of two of its more notable figures: Arizona Ranger Captain Burton C. Mossman in *Maverick Makers* (New York: Dutton, 1931) and Rurale Commandant Emilio Kosterlitzky in *Sheriff Killer* (New York: Dutton, 1932). Also, Mary Kidder Rak's *Border Patrol* (New York: Houghton Mifflin, 1938) relates a number of tales concerning that United States agency, which was the culmination of the earlier border law-enforcement institutions. Much of the same locale is gone over from the standpoint of the Apaches by Ross Santee in *Apache Land* (New York: Scribner's, 1947), while quite a different sort of culture and background is disposed of in the five short legendary Mexican tales related by Frank Goodwyn in *The Devil in Texas* (Dallas: Dealey & Lowe, 1936).

Within the periphery of border novels themselves, mention should be made of a couple of volumes that approximate the essential standards of general border literature but not of the border novel itself. Those are *Chaparral and Oranges* (San Antonio: Naylor, 1938) by Joe ("Blackie") Wilson, the background for which is the lower Rio Grande area; and Sarah Sanborne Weaver's *The White Buck: Legend of the Border* (San Antonio: Naylor, 1957), whose setting also is the international river in such towns as Mier and Rio Grande City and, more specifically, in Camargo, across the border in Tamaulipas. Of most recent vintage is Denise Chávez's *Loving Pedro Infante* (New York: Farrar,

Straus and Giroux, 2001), which is concerned with a fan club in a fictional border town near El Paso and devoted to the Mexican singing idol who died in 1957.

Certain other works of an autobiographical nature also should be called to mind, particularly Dr. Ira Jefferson Bush's account of his medical career, part of which was spent in the employ of legendary American landowner and mining magnate "Colonel" William Cornell Greene at Greene's celebrated fief in Sonora and which Bush related in *Gringo Doctor* (Caldwell, Idaho: Caxton Printers, 1939). And especially informative, too, is J. Frank Dobie's *A Vaquero of the Brush Country* (New York: Little, Brown, 1943), which is derived from the reminiscences of old-time South Texas cowman John Young. Even more noteworthy and valuable in its penetration of the magic curtain is Dobie's account of his one-year saddle trip through the north Mexican states of Coahuila, Chihuahua and parts of Durango and Zacatecas, which originally appeared as *Tongues of the Monte* in 1935 and later as *The Mexico I Like* (Dallas: Southern Methodist University Press, 1942).

Rather in the same vein is Dan de Lara Hughes' *South from Tombstone: A Life Story* (London: Methuen, 1938), which describes much of Hughes' early life and career near the turn of the century in mining and cattle operations in southern Arizona and northern Sonora. *South from Tombstone* is set in about the same background and times highlighted by the career of Jefferson Davis Milton, longtime border law enforcement officer whose story was told by J. Evetts Haley in *Jeff Milton: A Good Man With a Gun* (Norman: University of Oklahoma Press, 1948).

Fiction of the Border Country

Brown, James Cabell. *Calabazas; or Amusing Recollections of an Arizona "City"* (San Francisco: Valleau & Peterson, 1892).

Comfort, Will Levington. *Somewhere South in Sonora* (Boston: Houghton Mifflin, 1925).

Fergusson, Harvey. *The Conquest of Don Pedro* (New York: Pocket Books, 1954).

Fierro Blanco, Antonio de (pseud. of Walter Nordoff). *The Journey of the Flame* (Boston: Riverside Press, 1933).

Fuentes, Carlos. *The Old Gringo,* Margaret Sayers Peden and Carlos Fuentes, trans. (New York: Farrar, Straus & Giroux, 1985; and New York: Harper & Row [Perennial Library], 1986; originally published as *El gringo viejo,* México, D.F.: Fondo de Cultura Económica).

Garner, Claud. *Wetback* (New York: Coward, 1947).

Goodwyn, Frank. *The Magic of Limping John: A Story of the Mexican Border Country* (New York: Farrar & Rinehart, 1944).

______. *The Black Bull* (Garden City, New York: Doubleday, 1958).

Hinojosa, Rolando. *Partners in Crime* (Houston: Arte Público Press, 1985).

Irving, Clifford. *Tom Mix and Pancho Villa* (New York: St. Martin's Press, 1982).

Lea, Tom. *The Wonderful Country* (Boston: Little, Brown, 1957).

McCarthy, Cormac. *Blood Meridian, or, The Evening Redness in the West* (New York: Vintage, 1992).

______. *All the Pretty Horses* (New York: Vintage, 1993).

______. *The Crossing* (New York: Knopf, 1994).

______. *Cities of the Plain* (New York: Knopf, 1998).

McCoy, Ron[ald]. *Fandango* (Garden City, New York: Doubleday, 1984).

McMurtry, Larry. *Streets of Laredo* (New York: Simon & Schuster, 1993).

Nunn, Guy. *White Shadows* (New York: Reynal & Hitchcock, 1947).

Priddy, Laurance L. *Son of Durango* (Santa Fe: Sunstone Press, 1996).

Swarthout, Glendon. *They Came to Cordura* (New York: Random House, 1958).

Traven, B. *The Treasure of the Sierra Madre,* Basil Creighton, trans. (London: Chatto & Windus, 1934; New York: Knopf, 1935). English version revised by Bernard Smith.

______. *The Cotton-Pickers* (New York: Hill and Wang, 1969).

Selective Border Films in Chronological Order

Bordertown (1935). Vitaphone/Warner Bros., 100 minutes. Director: Archie Mayo. Cast: Paul Muni, Bette Davis, Margaret Lindsay, Eugene Pallette.

The Treasure of the Sierra Madre (1948). Warner Bros., 126 minutes. Director: John Huston. Cast: Humphrey Bogart, Walter Huston, Tim Holt, Alfonso Bedoya.

Border Incident (1949). Metro-Goldwyn-Mayer, 92 minutes. Director: Anthony Mann. Cast: Ricardo Montalban, George Murphy, Howard Da Silva, James Mitchell.

Borderline (1950). Universal International, 88 minutes. Director: William A. Seiter. Cast: Fred MacMurray, Claire Trevor, Raymond Burr, Roy Roberts.

Border River (1954). Universal International, 88 minutes. Director: George Sherman. Cast: Joel McCrea, Yvonne De Carlo, Pedro Armendariz, Alfonso Bedoya.

They Came to Cordura (1959). Columbia, 123 minutes. Director: Robert Rosen. Cast: Gary Cooper, Rita Hayworth, Van Heflin, Tab Hunter.

The Getaway (1972). Warner Bros., 122 minutes. Director: Sam Peckinpah. Cast: Steve McQueen, Ali MacGraw, Ben Johnson, Sally Struthers.

Goin' South (1978). Paramount, 101 minutes. Director: Jack Nicholson. Cast: Jack Nicholson, Mary Steenburgen, Christopher Lloyd, John Belushi.

Borderline (1980). Universal, 97 minutes. Director: Jerrold Freeman. Cast: Charles Bronson, Bruno Kirby, Burt Remsen, Ed Harris.

The Border (1982). Universal, 109 minutes. Director: Tony Richardson. Cast: Jack Nicholson, Harvey Keitel, Valerie Perrine, Warren Oates.

The Old Gringo (1989). Columbia, 120 minutes. Director: Luis Puenzo. Cast: Gregory Peck, Jane Fonda, Jimmy Smits, Pedro Armendariz, Jr.

El Mariachi (1992). Columbia, 78 minutes. Director: Robert Rodriguez. Cast: Carlos M. Gallardo, Consuelo Gomez, Jaime de Hoyos, Peter Marquardt.

Mountains, Mists and Mexico (1995). Documentary film. Bandana Productions, 56 minutes.

Touch of Evil (1998, restored version; initial release 1958). Universal, 108 minutes; 111 minutes. Director: Orson Welles. Cast: Charlton Heston, Janet Leigh, Orson Welles, Marlene Dietrich.

Streets of Laredo (1999). Television mini-series; two episodes, based on Larry McMurtry's novel of the same name, with co-writer Diana Ossana; 300 minutes. Director: Joseph Sargent. Cast: James Garner, Cissy Spacek, Ned Beatty, George Carlin.

All the Pretty Horses (2000). Columbia/Miramar, 117 minutes. Director: Billy Bob Thornton. Cast: Matt Damon, Henry Thomas, Penelope Cruz, Lucas Black.

Traffic (2000). USA Films, 117 minutes. Director: Steven Soderbergh. Cast: Benicio Del Toro, Jacob Vargas, Michael Douglas, Erika Christensen.

Index